LIFE – NOW AND HEREAFTER

By the same author:

Bridges - Ancient Wisdom Revealed
Hardcover: ISBN 978-3-929345-11-7
Paperback: ISBN 978-3-929345-32-2

All is Relative – A Revelation of Man's Cosmic
Connections
ISBN 978-3-929345-21-6

Aart Jurriaanse

LIFE
NOW
AND
HEREAFTER

On the Nature of
Life and Death

BRIDGES
PUBLISHING

First Published in South Africa 1987 as a private publication by the author.

The publisher of this re-edition wishes to acknowledge the support of Pat.

© 2007 by the "Sun Centre" School of Esoteric Philosophy, South Africa

Cover by Rosi Weiss
Typography by Hans-Jürgen Maurer

Published 2007 by:
Bridges Publishing
Hans-Juergen Maurer
Poststr. 3
79098 Freiburg
Germany

in Cooperation with:
"Sun Centre"
School of Esoteric Philosophy
5, Almond Drive
Somerset West 7130
South Africa

www.verlaghjmaurer.de

info@verlaghjmaurer.de

ISBN 978-3-929345-25-4

The Tibetan

1. "There is no death. There is, as you know, entrance into fuller life. There is freedom from the handicaps of the fleshly vehicle." (4-300)

2. "Perhaps as (students' study and read and think (on the subject of death), material of interest will come their way which could be gradually assembled and published." (4-302)

3. "I conjure all of you to push the study of death and its technique as far as possible and to carry forward (esoteric) investigation of this matter." (4-507)

4. "The release of a soul through disease and death is not necessarily an unhappy occurrence. A new and better attitude to the phenomenon of death is essential, is possible and near." (17-350)

5. "It is also my hope that students will do something of major importance to aid in bringing forth the light upon the processes of death which humanity is today demanding." (17-410)

(For references see Appendix).

"Who makes you, my friend, so important?
What do you possess that was not given you?
If then you really received it all as a gift,
Why take the credit to yourself?"
1 Cor. 4:7

Publisher's Note

In the first edition of this book (1987), Aart Jurriaanse quotes longer passages from the following titles, comprising 100 pages of his own book:

1.) Jasper Swain, *On the Death of My Son*. This book was also published under the titles *Mike*, in which the author appears under the pseudonym "Ronald Norman", and *From my world to yours*. A 1997 edition of this book is titled *Heaven's Gift: Conversations from Beyond the Veil*.

2.) Dr. George Lindsay Johnson, *The Great Problem and the Evidence for its Solution*

3.) Helen Greaves, *Testimony of Light*

The publisher regrets that the quotes taken from these books had to be omitted for this new, 2007 edition. However, we encourage the reader to obtain copies of these current editions as the author found these books to offer very valuable accounts of the after-life states.

CONTENTS

INTRODUCTION

The trouble in composing a book of this nature is to know where to start and what to include. The subject itself covers a very broad scope and furthermore there is such a wide range of readers for whom to cater, with each individual at his own specific level of emotional, intellectual and spiritual development.

There are those who, during the course of their lives, have accumulated extensive academic knowledge in certain fields of study, but because their attention has been focused within the relatively narrow boundaries of their particular terrain of investigation, they have become specialists on their subjects, but have nevertheless acquired only a limited general knowledge. There are also those with a wide knowledge of the material world, but who know next to nothing about the subjective spheres, and are hardly aware of the existence of the vast worlds of the spirit by which they are constantly surrounded. There are the religious minded who from early childhood have been trained in the precepts of some particular religion, the nature of which frequently largely depends on their country of birth or the nation to which they belong. Such religious training is usually founded on dogmatic teachings which members of such a denomination are supposed to believe, to accept blindly and without too much reflection on or analysis of the propounded tenets.

Then there are those who, owing to life's circumstances, have not been favoured with extensive scholastic education, but who nevertheless may have been imbued with an effective common sense, a sound sense of values and discrimination, or what may be termed an innate wisdom, which quite often may serve a much more useful purpose for the proper understanding of these concepts than actual academic training.

Lastly, and unfortunately the group to which probably the majority of mankind still belongs, there are those whose mental capacity is still largely dormant and who merely apply their intelligence for satisfying their needs, their lusts, desire and selfish emotional and physical greed, but who, as yet, have hardly become aware of the deeper aspects of life and have not yet learnt to direct their thoughts towards that which is noble and sublime. This applies to the unthinking masses, the bulk of the supporters of the many religions, those of the electoral mob who are either incapable or otherwise too indolent to think for themselves and to formulate their own conclusions. These individuals are as a rule readily swayed by the plausible and usually emotional words of the religious or political orator, or the agitator in revolt against the ruling establishment.

The thoughts to be expressed are relatively elementary, depending on the point of approach of the reader. They contain nothing new as they form part of the principles of the Ancient Wisdom teachings, which have been at man's disposal for thousands of years – that is to those who have been ready for them. So far only comparatively small numbers have, however, been aware of, or have shown any real interest in the proclaimed principles.

As will be stressed over and over again in the following pages, these studies leave a very wide scope for individual interpretation of the Truth, and of the Path that can be followed, because each individual person must find his own specific level in accordance with his own particular characteristics and the ever changing circumstances brought about by his karmic destiny and the fortunes of life.

The approach to be followed is purely philosophical or metaphysical, and not in support of any particular school of thought or religion. Readers are therefore asked to weigh and consider the different principles that are propounded strictly objectively, thus enabling them to arrive at their own independent conclusions. What is important however, is that man should learn to apply his independent thought to these matters and to break away from relatively futile dogmatic teachings which have largely become outdated, and have to a considerable extent been responsible for the lack of interest display in present day church life. Please not that this does not imply a lack of interest in religious thought or in matters which concern the spirit. If concepts are to prove worthwhile they must, however, remain vital and sparkling, and to retain such vigour they should keep on growing and must constantly be adapted to keep pace with the demands of the ever changing and evolving human race. Therefore, with regard to spiritual matters, never allow your approach to become stagnant and sterile. Continue thinking and pondering on available facts and ideas, ever trying to penetrate deeper into the surrounding and unrevealed secrets of the great Unknown.

All that is demanded of man is that he should strive to live in accordance with the highest moral and spiritual standards of which he may be aware at his particular stage of development. For this purpose he should as far as possible make every endeavour to suppress those purely natural human inclinations which tend towards a selfish approach to life. He should therefore do his best to promote improved human relationships by goodwill, understanding, and by sharing the gifts of life with which he has been favoured, whether these concern his physical, emotional, mental or spiritual relationships with his fellow men.

As the Ancient Wisdom covers the whole spectrum of human endeavour, attention for present purposes will be focused mainly on one aspect, namely trying to gain a somewhat clearer insight into what becomes of the soul or spirit after the occurrence of physical death.

The average man has only a vague or confused idea of what may be expected. Although many churches no longer stress the dreaded agonies and perpetual suffering in purgatory, this nagging apprehension is inclined to remain at the back of the mind of many "sinners". In many instances these ideas have been firmly imprinted in their minds since early childhood, and it is difficult to rid themselves entirely of this tormenting fear. The only effective way of eventually attaining peace of mind to some extent, is to arrive at a clearer understanding of the nature of the Hereafter, and what reasonably may be expected to happen after death of the physical vehicle.

Since the Hereafter is a most relative concept, and is experienced in the elusive, intangible and invisible etheric spheres which man, while still confined to his physical body, cannot readily conceived and understand, it is not surprising that representations thereof will vary considerably. This is further accentuated and complicated by the fact that this future abode, especially while still located in the astral spheres, will apparently vary for each individual according to his particular state of consciousness, his experiences and stage of development. No wonder that no two descriptions of what may be expected will therefore be in perfect agreement, because it will all depend on the specific outlook of the particular observer who is describing conditions, and furthermore the interpretation of any such description will also depend on the mental level attained by the student concerned.

Today a wide range of esoteric literature is actually at the disposal of the interested student, and although many variations with regard to detail are bound to occur in these descriptions, a considerable measure of correspondence concerning the underlying principles will nevertheless become evident.

From what is to follow it will also become apparent that the nature of life which may be expected to be experienced in the Hereafter, will in the first instance depend on the activities and mental attitude during the present life in the phenomenal world. In **Part I** an attempt will therefore be made to present a brief survey of the nature of man with the idea of providing a somewhat clearer understanding of his being. In due course this might then induce him to take the necessary steps which will eventually ensure a better and more effective life on earth, thus automatically preparing him for a correspondingly more harmonious and complete after-life.

For a description of the conditions which may be expected to be encountered on the other side of the veil, it has been decided to use certain extracts from independent sources, which to some extent may be regarded as representative of current literature.

For this purpose the bible was considered in the first instance. This widely accepted guide to spiritual matters actually, however, provides relatively little specific information as to exactly what may be expected when we pass over. Nevertheless a number of texts, directly or indirectly concerned with this subject, have been selected. (See Part I: 9. Biblical Perspectives.)

In Part II of the book a further brief survey of the Master Djwhal Khul's teachings has been set out, dealing more specifically with the nature of earth and some aspects of what may be expected in the life hereafter.

PART I

THE NATURE AND PURPOSE OF EXISTENCE

For clearer understanding of the nature of Life and Death, the reader should at least be aware of some of the basic principles on which human existence, whether considered from the standpoint of the phenomenal world or that of the realms of spirit, are founded. These concepts or Laws of Nature will only be briefly dealt with in order to provide a general framework for the principles involved, and thereby contributing towards a better understanding of the life experiences which may be described or encountered.

1

NATURE REMAINS IN
A PERPETUAL STATE OF CHANGE

All that IS, whether atom, planet or spirit, consists of ENERGY. This vital and divine force has been incorporated by the Creator into an infinite variety of form, both tangible and intangible, and organised with the object of eventually achieving some Divine Purpose and Plan, the nature of which ranges totally beyond the conception of the limited human mind.

The Rays of Energy originating from the Primordial source, have during their passage through Universal Space already traversed the spheres of influence of several higher constellations or heavenly bodies, and have thus been modified considerably in quality and mitigated in potency by the time they reach our Solar system, and finally our relatively minute habitat, the planet Earth. Although these Rays of energy vary considerably in quality and in their effect on the bodies subjected to irradiation, they have one characteristic in common, and that is that all energy remains in a state of perpetual motion, never coming to rest. To the deceptive and imperfect human perception it might for instance appear that the energy invested and locked up in a mineral or rock, perhaps already for thousands of years, is something that is dead, inert and totally inactive. This, however, is not the case, and fortunately present day scientists have now also become aware of the fact that the energy contained in each and every atom of creation, whether that atom happens to be temporarily contained in a mineral, a plant or an animal body, it remains vitally alive and in a constant state of motion or circulation. This atomic movement is, in fact, not securely confined by the outer walls of the atom, because a certain amount of percolation or interchange of energy is constantly taking place by energy escaping through the enclosing atom wall. This escaping energy is, however, still being attracted and held by the cohesive magnetic power of the inner energy and thus forms a secondary mantle of energy, known as the "etheric body", by which each atom or any other material body composed of multiple collections of atoms is surrounded.

But as is the case with the energy contained within the atom, that which serves to form its etheric surround, also remains in perpetual and vital circulation, exchanging its force not only with the enclosed atom, but also with the etheric field of immediately adjoining atoms with which it happens to be in contact.

The etheric surround of the atom serves several functions. The contained energy may either react positively or negatively in respect of neighbouring atoms, thus having a magnetic or repulsive effect as the case may be. Where the effect is magnetic, atoms are mutually attracted and adhere together to form molecules. Each of these groups of atoms again disposing of their own reconstructed and combined etheric surround, which serves as the binding element for cementing such atomic or molecular units together for building the various forms demanded by Nature.

Each and every form therefore not only has its *etheric body*, but this outer surround is again intimately linked with those of adjoining atoms, thus forming an inner etheric network, penetrating right down to basic atomic levels. Apart from the cohesive properties of the etheric structure, it fulfils a further important function by simultaneously serving as a channel of contact whereby the energies temporarily restricted to from, remain in constant touch and integration, not only with immediately surrounded energy patterns, but with all the energy contained within the Universe, and thus eventually with the Supernal Power. It should be noted that the etheric network therefore serves as a two-way channel for energy reactions – on the one hand energy vibrations or influences are transferred from outer spheres of influence down to atom levels, and at the same time any reactions experienced by the atom or its combinations, are again reflected and communicated via the etheric system to outer spheres.

Yes, what a magnificent system of inconceivable grandeur, of which the average person remains totally unaware and of which the thinker can only begin to form some faint conception!

It is therefore by means of Energy and its etheric network that all of creation, considered from the atomic, planetary and cosmic points of view, and including both the phenomenal and spiritual, is synthesized into the Universal ONE.

These concepts of which only the fringes have been touched in this superficial survey, contain several additional implications. Of these it is felt that at least one further aspect should be stressed, and that is the Energy must be regarded as synonymous with Life. Therefore, if ALL consists of Energy, then every form of Creation also contains Life, even though such Life cannot always be discerned by dull human perception.

The difference between the multiple patterns of Life of which the Universe is constituted, merely lies in the degree of activity and consciousness that is exhibited. It is mainly on these differences that the human being has founded his artificial classification of the several kingdoms of nature of which the lowest, the mineral kingdom, is regarded by the majority as being totally inane and lifeless. From the Ancient Wisdom point of view, however, this is certainly not the case, as the minerals are actually vibrant with Life, but of a Life which, according to human interpretation, has not yet become consciously aware of itself.

One of the conclusions to which these thoughts must inevitably lead, is that if all that is consists of vital Energy, which remains in constant movement, then nothing that exists can be regarded as absolutely stable and immutable. And such in fact is the position – every form or appearance, of whatever pattern, system or nature, remains in a perpetual state of change and adaptation and this proceeds from moment to moment, hour to hour, year to year, and age to age, and is never ending because both Energy and Life endure as part of the recognisable attributes of the ONE LIFE.

These energy changes may be referred to as being in a state of:

Involution – representing the stage of primary absorption of energy during the process of constructive building of new forms of life, or

Evolution – where changes are effected to existing forms to adapt these to more effective or productive use to meet the demands of the ever-changing surround and circumstances. Finally a stage is reached which might be called

Devolution – referring to the destructive process of breaking down existing forms, which have served their purpose, into simpler components, thus allowing such elements to become available for regrouping into subsequent forms demanded by Nature. In other instances the composing energy which has temporarily been restricted, may be released altogether to be re-absorbed into the cosmic energy reservoir to continue its interminable functions in illimitable Eternity.

And thus mankind, as part of the universal complex of Nature, is also subject to these same laws of perpetual change and evolution. Man has evolved from some unknown Source and during the course of aeons has attained his present phase of development on an insignificant little planet, which represents but a fleeting instant in his interminable destiny.

This also applies to the individual, whose perishable mortal body, subject to the laws of inheritance, has been derived from primitive ancestors. But even in the present life this material body remains obedient to the many Laws of Nature, the laws of physical growth and development, starting from the moment of conception in the mother's womb and followed by the birth of the child, its maturing, then later the years of physical decline, ultimately ending with the death and disintegration of this temporary vehicle of the soul. This material human body has simultaneously, and during every stage of its laborious progress been surrounded by its etheric replica. Furthermore, closely synchronised with the *physical* development, there was a corresponding unfoldment of the intangible *emotional* and *mental bodies*, which aspects remain intimately associated with and really form an integral part of the discernable physical system. All these bodies, from moment to moment and year to year, and whether in the process of growth or decline, remain in a perpetual state of change and adaptation.

As will be discussed in somewhat greater detail under a subsequent heading, the material bodies referred to above are, however, incomplete without the cohesive and directly spiritual element of the *immortal Soul*, availing itself of the phenomenal aspects as vehicles of expression, and as instruments for gaining the needed experience in the world of matter. What is of importance with regard to the present context, is that the Soul, this inner being, the real source of consciousness, also remains in a condition of constant adjustment, learning from gained experience and progressively evolving, not only in this one life, but in fact from life to life during the course of ages, moving through innumerable re-incarnations, and thus gradually finding its way back on the Path of Return, back to its Origin – back to the House of the Father.

2

THE DUALITY OF MAN

No true concept of the nature of human existence can be conceived until man can gain a somewhat clearer picture of the essence of his own constitution.

To the uninformed, man is no more than that physical appearance perceptible to the eye; a mortal body born from its mother's womb, and undergoing the processes of growth and development. Eventually, depending on the fortunes of life and an infinite range of circumstances, he will experience the many vicissitudes of joy and sorrow which serve to complete the pattern of each individual destiny. The length of such a life may vary from anything between a few minutes to over a hundred years, and will be characterised in varying degree by the weals and woes of fate. Some individuals undoubtedly experience a heavier share of affliction than others and are apparently rewarded with only a minimum of happiness. On the other hand it should be remembered that none can traverse this "vale of tears" without his just share of pain and agony, because it is only through such trials and reverses that life's lessons are step by step being learned.

The degree of misery to which man is exposed will, however, largely be determined by his own activities and attitudes towards life, not only during his present span of being, but also during that of previous incarnations. Yes, it is all a question of cause and effect, and man can depend on it that what is commonly known as fate, whether good or bad, is merely his just reward eventuating from thoughts or deeds of the past.

Mention has been made above about previous lives, about reincarnation and evolution of the individual during the course of ages.

How can all this be identified with the death and disintegration of the substantial body at the termination of a specific span of mortal life? The explanation of this enigma is fairly simple once the underlying principles are understood. Man is a duality, consisting of a tangible and perishable material body, which serves as a temporary vehicles or instrument for an impalpable and immortal indwelling Soul or Spirit. At "death" the Soul is withdrawn from the vehicle, which has served its purpose as a channel of experience and expression for a particular life period, and is now released for a while from material bondage to continue its development in subjective spheres.

Simultaneously with the escape of the Soul, the life-thread is also withdrawn from the substantial body, which means that the latter has lost the cohesive power which served to synthesize the various constituent elements. The result is that decomposition will set in and that the recognisable human form will in due course disintegrate.

Notwithstanding the periodic death and demolition of the substantial form of the individual, the progressive evolution of the material existence of the human race as a whole is sustained and achieved by means of its physical propagation and the transmitting of specific qualities to posterity by means of the chromosomes contained within the male and female reproductive cells. This will ensure that the evolving soul will also be enabled to occupy systematically improved vehicles for its future enhanced requirements during subsequent reincarnations.

The mortal physical body is actually a far more complicated structure than is commonly appreciated. The purely physical aspect only forms part of a larger complex, usually known as the "*Personality*", which also includes the more ephemeral astral and mental aspects. It is the function of the Soul to co-ordinate and bring these three aspects of the personality to significant expression.

The position would perhaps be more readily understood if outlined schematically:

I.   **The Personality** (or lower Self) is composed of

1.   The **physical** body, consisting of
   (a)   the *etheric* or *vital* body,
   (b)   the *dense physical* aspect.
   2. The *emotional* or *astral* body.
   3. The *mental* body, including the *lower concrete mind*.

When referring to the astral and mental "bodies", this expression should not be interpreted too literally, as the relative "bodies" are merely represented by surrounding spheres of influence where the energies concerned are focused and interact, producing effects which impel and direct the associated physical body.

II.   **The Soul** (or higher Self)

This is not a "body" in the accepted sense, but the linking principle between Matter and Spirit, or the Christ Principle serving as a tie between God and one of His innumerable manifestations in form.

   The highest aspect of the Soul is known as the *Higher* or *Abstract Mind*, which represents the link between the Soul and …

III.   **The Spiritual Triad**

This is the triple reflection of the *Monad*, through which the Father functions at lower levels. Expression is gained through:
   1. the *Spiritual Will*,
   2. the *Intuition*, *Love-Wisdom*, the *Christ-Principle*, and
   3. the *Higher* or *Abstract Mind*.

On a higher level the Triad stands in the same relationship to the Monad, as the Personality stands to the Soul – the lower serving as instrument for the higher.

IV.   **The Monad**

This is Pure Spirit, the Father in Whom the Divine Triplicity is reflected as:
   1. *Divine Will* or *Power* .the Father
   2. *Love-Wisdom* . . . . .the Son
   3. *Active Intelligence* . . . . .the Holy Spirit

Direct or conscious contact between the Monad (the Triad) and personality is only effected when man is nearing the end of his journey of experience in the three lower worlds, and when the gap in consciousness between Spirit and Matter has been bridged by the 'Lighted Way'. At this stage the personality therefore becomes a direct instrument of service under direction of the Monad. This means that the Soul is now being by-passed or superseded, and thus having fulfilled its arduous task over the course of millennia and during innumerable incarnations, it will gradually lose its identity by being absorbed in the more comprehensive constitution of the Monad of which it has always formed a vital component.

Unity, duality or triplicities are in fact all merely facets of the same concept, representing different approaches and points of view, which largely depend on the unfolding consciousness.

The awakening aspirant becomes aware of many aspects of *duality*; he beings to differentiate more distinctly between good and evil, between personality and Soul, and between matter and Spirit.

Manifestation may, however, also be regarded as a *triplicity*: Life-Quality-Form or expressed in different terms, as Spirit-Soul-Body. But all these are merely inadequate attempts to express in words various aspects of Deity, of which man might be vaguely aware, but which he will never be able to fully comprehend. These triplicities are therefore only facets of a *Unity* which man has identified under the inclusive name of GOD.

To the aspirant his existence may be largely interpreted in terms of duality or opposites, and these pairs of opposites meet on the emotional or astral plane, where they act and interact and where these clashes may develop into major conflicts. In reality the battle is a struggle for dominance waged between the soul and its vehicle, matter, manifested as the personality. The average man, however, remains unaware of this underlying conflict and of the issues involved; he is only concerned with the lesser or secondary activities, such as the struggle between light and darkness, good and evil, pleasure and pain, freedom and suppression, poverty and riches, and many more.

Before an aspirant can begin to work effectively with world forces and problems, he first has to balance the opposites in his own system.

When this equilibrium has to some extent been achieved, he has entered the Path and can now become a co-worker in the wider field.

To the little evolved there are as yet no problems of duality, as these individuals still remain unaware of anything beyond the world of matter. The aspirant, however, becomes aware of opposites, and this leaves him stranded, vague and uncertain somewhere in between, being pulled hither and thither by the dual poles. The man who is thus becoming aware of the presence of the Soul, realises that he is suspended between two forces – the attraction of matter or form, as opposed to that of the Soul. It is this double attraction accentuating the many dualities, which brings the aspirant to the recognition that his own divine will, as opposed to the selfish will of his personality, constitutes the deciding factor. Through the light he has found, he has become aware of the darkness; he sees the good as his ideal, but the urge of the flesh draws him towards evil; he experiences hell on Earth and consequently aspires towards a spiritual heaven as his sanctuary.

These dual forces may be seen as two streams of energy or two paths leading in opposite directions – the one back to material selfish desire, associated with the dreary cycle of rebirth, and the other to the freedom of the world of souls.

For the aspirant who has relatively made only recent conscious contact with his inner guide, there usually follow years of severe strain and struggle. He has repeatedly to face the opposites, and decisions and choices have to be made. He comes to realise that he can no longer continue along the way of least resistance. From time to time he obtains flashes of insight and new visions appear to him, only to be engulfed again by the requirements of everyday life and the selfish desires and demands of the personality. Another consideration which may play an appreciable role, is the fear of ridicule by relations and friends who have not yet become aware of these deeper perceptions, or else refuse to acknowledge these experiences. It may require very strong convictions to overcome such fears or even active opposition, and to proceed calmly along the way, disregarding all disparagement and opprobrium.

Once the striver has reached the point of decision, and has turned his footsteps to the Light, he will find that active support will be forthcoming from both the Soul and certain subjective Entities who are always ready and willing to reach out a helping hand. Should his resolve, however, weaken or his energies flag, then he will *temporarily* revert to the old habits and conditions of the unawakened man, with murky clouds and glamours of the astral plane settling over him again. This only means that these same battles will have to be waged anew, until he finally succeeds in meeting these challenges.

To speak of 'final attainment' and 'final destination' is of course paradoxical, because everything in our Universe is relative and 'finality' can never be achieved in an infinite Universe. Progress only means moving from one point of attainment to the next, from initiation to initiation, from one plane of consciousness to a higher, and so ever on and on, higher and higher, until …?

But to return to Earth – should the aspirant's path lead him to higher levels, then this will mean new expansions of consciousness, fresh revelations, deeper understanding, a more comprehensive grasp of the realities of life, and simultaneously new challenges to be surmounted. New powers and capacities will be evoked, and new fields of experience and service will be disclosed to him, and all this will be attended by increased responsibilities.

While embracing the inner relationships and subjective attitudes of the higher aspects of a dual life, the candidate remains faced with the fact that he is still standing in the outer physical life, entailing certain commitments and responsibilities which may not be lightly ignored. His problem is to stand spiritually free while surrounded by his worldly obligations; to function in subjective realms, and yet to continue his activities in the world of human experience; to attain true spiritual detachment while simultaneously rendering due service to his fellow men.

3

THE SOUL

Under the previous heading mention has been made of the Soul, which may be regarded as the dual and immortal aspect of the human being. For gaining a clearer understanding of this ephemeral constituent and rather elusive concept, a closer acquaintance is therefore needed of its nature and functions.

The individual Soul may be regarded as a spark or minute expression of the One Soul, the spiritual aspect of God. This is therefore the factor which determines that which is divine in every human being, and induces the qualities of life and consciousness. In the unevolved the presence of this Inner Guide, the Spiritual Self or Christ Principle, may largely remain hidden and unrecognised, while still being shrouded and dominated by the material urges and lower impulses of the flesh. Rest assured, however, that this indwelling Flame is present in each and every individual and is only biding its time gradually gaining ascendancy over the personality aspects and asserting itself by guiding the individual towards his higher destiny. This evolutionary process is, as a rule, however extremely slow and tedious, and will be spread over many lives.

It is the presence of the soul that distinguishes man from the animal, and it was only when animal-man became endowed with his own Soul that he was "individualised" and raised from the animal to the human kingdom of nature. The Soul is the factor which invests man with self-consciousness. It is the element responsible for the absorption and assimilation of life's experiences and for transmitting the essence of such gained experience from incarnation to incarnation.

It is by means of the attribute of immortality that the Soul ensures not only the continuity of individual existence, but as the transmitter of the cumulative effect of experience in the sustained process of reincarnation, it also provides the necessary facilities for persistent spiritual growth and evolution.

The concept of the soul is something so vague and intangible that it simply cannot be clearly or adequately defined. It is only when man becomes aware of this indwelling Self within his own being that he will gradually achieve a better understanding of the nature of this Inner Director.

Normally those people who are prepared to go to the trouble of thoughtful self-examination to obtain some conception of the functioning of their being, fortunately do become aware of the fact of conflicting inner forces. As a rule this is brought to expression by the inclination to satisfy the urges of the flesh or of selfish greed, which then comes into conflict with an opposing and more altruistic disposition to direct thoughts or activities not solely towards personal well-being, but also to consider the interests of fellow men. That means that their thoughts are inspired by goodwill, consideration and loving understanding. This proneness to react to the loftier leanings instead of the baser and more self-seeking tendencies of the lower nature, originate from the Christ Principle by which the soul is characterised.

Many, although aware of these inner struggles, have not consciously recognised the deeper implications of these experiences, and that these clashes between opposing inclinations of the personality are in fact indications that the Soul is beginning to assert its influence. In the majority of instances this is so merely because the persons concerned have not yet reached the stage where this inner constitution of their being has become of active interest to them, and they consequently have not yet devoted any serious thought to the subject. Others again are so involved in the struggle of achieving success in the several fields of the material world of human competition, in gaining substantial riches, in satisfying the desires and emotions and gathering knowledge that might prove useful for attaining their ambitious objectives, that they cannot afford the time to ponder on the deeper and spiritual aspects of life. In a way this seems most regrettable, but it should be remembered that this is merely the normal course of life, during which each individual Soul remains in a constant state of development, and must necessarily pass through every possible phase of experience which life in the phenomenal world has to offer, including both the good and the bad, the bitter and the sweet. It is from these experiences that the Soul is steadily learning, and is step by step gaining in wisdom.

The Soul is neither spirit nor matter, but represents the divine principle by which these two extremes are being related. It is the element providing individual Life with its qualities and characteristics and latent powers of expression. It is the source of self-consciousness, and the channel for registering conscious awareness of the environment. The extent to which the consciousness is expanding is therefore an indication of the progressive integration of the Soul with its instrument of expression, and of the measure to which it is taking command of vital decisions. The Soul furthermore represents the principles of sentiency and intelligence in man, which are demonstrated as mental awareness and are the expressions of the discriminative Higher Mind.

EGOIC LOTUS

In esoteric literature reference is often made to the "Egoic Lotus". In this symbolic and most apt comparison the Soul is represented as a jewel situated in the heart of a lotus, being enclosed by nine petals of the flower, arranged in three concentric whorls, each containing three petals. In the early stages of development the flower is still in the closed bud stage, with the petals tightly enfolding and hiding the jewel in its centre. With progressive spiritual development the individual petals systematically begin to unfold as life follows life, and experience, discrimination, understanding, love and wisdom are gradually being acquired. As these petals slowly unfold, one after another, they begin to radiate their beautiful colour and light. By the time man is approaching human perfection, and the Soul is therefore nearing the termination of its cyclic earthly career, the nine petals will finally be fully unfolded, exposing the radiating jewel at its centre, with its surrounding colourful petals in the full glory of its exquisite beauty.

Apparently the splendour of such a fully unfolded egoic lotus is simply beyond description, providing its fortunate instrument with that lustre and brilliance, radiated as sparkling streams of energy from the ceaselessly vibrating flower. Every petal is like a quivering point of fire, and this vital life is reflected and accentuated by the scintillating jewel at its centre. The streams of energy radiating from the flowing lotus will not only serve to illumine the vehicle temporarily occupied, but may also be directed towards any other outer objective for achieving some constructive purpose.

A further symbolic description is used when reference is sometimes made to the "*Causal Body*" or the "*Temple of the Soul*". This is the figurative vehicle of the Soul, with neither definite shape nor form, serving as its divine storehouse, where the essence of life, the good and valuable, garnered from the endless experiences of innumerable lives, has been accumulated and stored. It therefore serves as a central receiving and transmission station. This causal body forms part of the essential equipment of the Soul, departing with the soul at the conclusion of each physical life, eventually to accompany the Soul again on its next venture into flesh.

SOUL ATTRIBUTES

During the later evolutionary stages the presence of the soul may be readily detected by some of its outstanding characteristics. As a rule the soul-infused being will be identified by such qualities as *altruism, wisdom, idealism, group service, sound discrimination, understanding, sacrifice, inclusiveness, willingness to share, impersonality, perseverance, compassion, self-control, steadfast love* and *goodwill*, and the calm, flexible but determined purpose of the spiritual Self. These properties may be contrasted with those so typically prone to be encountered in the uncontrolled personality, such as *selfishness* in its many forms, *greed, lust, desire, hate, spitefulness, anger, sensuousness, pride, ambition, dominance, unreasonableness* and *injustice*. These latter traits must step by step be conquered and subdued during the course of time by the opposing Soul features before the conflict will be finally terminated.

The extent to which the following qualities are brought to expression in daily life will not only be an indication of the presence of the Soul, but will also denote to what degree the Inner Ruler is attaining ascendancy over the baser inclinations of the personality.

29

(i) **Light**

Several types of light may be distinguished, such as the light of matter, the light of instinct, the light of knowledge or of the lower mind, the light of the Higher Mind or the Soul, and finally the light of Intuition or of Spirit.

The extent to which the Soul has taken command of its vehicle, will immediately become apparent to the informed by the subjective Light radiated by the individual. Once the seeker has distinguished the first glimmering signs of Light within himself, he also becomes aware of the contrasting surrounding darkness. At first this may lead to despair and depression, but eventually these dark shadows will be dispersed by the growing Light of the Soul. This will mean the introduction of a totally new phase in his life, illumined by the glory of an ever brighter burning Inner Flame. This Inner Light will lead the aspirant to a growing Soul consciousness and the Path of Light. By treading this Path, he himself becomes a source of Light, bringing inspiration to his fellow men.

It will be found that the practical use of the available light will in due course not deplete the source, but will in fact increase its radiance, thus constantly leading to new revelations and the recognition of the beauties of life formerly hidden by the murky shadows of matter and ignorance.

(ii) **Intuition**

In the soul-infused man the faculty of intuition will be awakened in ever increasing proportions, thus unfailingly leading him to right decision and action on behalf of others. It must be noted, however, that the intuition referred to is not the emotionally motivated 'intuition' which might be implied by the uninformed. No, true intuition is something totally different, is spiritually inspired, and will guide the skilled performer unerringly to his objective. The average man, still mainly centred in his personality, and not yet truly aware of the Light of the Soul, should therefore not yet rely too much on so-called intuition, but should instead much rather depend on his normal intellect, the 'common-sense' of the mind. This lower form of 'intuition' in the majority of instances originates from astral levels and can therefore not be relied upon as it might easily lead him astray.

Although the higher form of intuition is normally associated with relatively advanced spiritual workers, it will however also begin to make its periodic appearance at an earlier stage, especially in instances where the aspirant finds himself under critical circumstances, or when help is urgently invoked on behalf of others.

As the worker progressively comes under stronger Soul control, he will find that he increasingly avails himself of intuitive decisions characterised by their swiftness and infallibility, instead of the far more elaborate and slower mental processes, which so often remain subject to error and illusion.

(iii) Love and Goodwill

These two attributes are closely related, as *goodwill* is in fact merely one of the expressions of *Love*, going hand in hand with such other facets as *kindness, harmlessness, understanding, forgiveness, sacrifice, humility* and *compassion*. All these are but variations of the Energy of Love, with the accent focused on some particular aspect. The quality of Love, with its many facets of expression, is characteristic of the soul and will provide an infallible criterion for determining the extent to which the Soul has already taken charge of the personality.

Love is however a most relative concept, and might be broadly classified into physical, emotional, mental and eventually spiritual or divine love. Where Love is referred to in the present context without further qualification, it is this latter and higher form of Love that will be implied. In its early stages of manifestation in the personality, it is at first of an entirely selfish nature, and as a rule sensually or emotionally orientated. As Soul influence progressively becomes more pronounced, so will the nature of the love expressed, be transformed, changing from the original self-love to love of a life partner, love of the family, and thus gradually unfolding to the ever wider sphere of group love, until it eventually will embrace all of humanity and creation – love of the Divine Source. The Energy of Love is thus responsible for bringing all the beautiful and harmonious aspects of the Soul into outer expression.

Goodwill is more specifically the art of directing the energies of Light, Love and Understanding to all men. Once these qualities become the keynotes of life, it changes the whole outlook and personality of all concerned, and must inevitably result in improved relationships and more harmonious conditions.

(iv) Serenity

The Soul-inspired individual will be characterised by deep serenity, an inner calm and enduring patience. This is because the Soul, aware of its immortality, knows steadfast persistence.

Serenity should not be confused with peace, which is a relative and temporary condition in a constantly changing world. To effect progress, peaceful circumstances must inevitably be disturbed. Peace refers to a state of feeling and emotion, whereas inner serenity pertains to the Soul and could be maintained even amidst violent disturbances in the three worlds of the personality – the physical, emotional and mental spheres.

Serenity, on the other hand, should certainly not be regarded as insensitivity. It is in fact a state of intense feeling which has been transmuted by the Soul into the repose of deep understanding. The Soul-centred individual will reach the stage where nothing will be able to disturb his inner calm, based upon his knowledge of and absolute reliance on the Supernal Powers by which he is controlled, and which are steadily directing him towards his higher destiny. His serenity will be expressed as perfect poise and equilibrium.

Joy and serenity are as a rule closely linked, clearly indicating by their presence that such a life is under direction of the Soul.

(v) Joy

A distinction should be made between joy and happiness. The latter remains a personality reaction and is based on the satisfying of desire, feeling and emotion. Being founded on the unstable emotional aspects of life, happiness is subject to the many disturbances of the environment and will thus fluctuate between the heights of delight and the depths of misery and depression.

Those who seek to live as Souls will eventually however experience the far deeper quality and stability of joy. There is the joy of reaching the objective after struggle, strain and pain; the joy or revelling in the Light after seemingly endless struggling in the dark; the joy of achievement and subsequent temporary peace, after striving and wrestling against opposing forces; the joy of achieving Soul contact with a kindred spirit; the joy of self-realisation; the joy of hours well spent in helping some fellow man, and contributing towards the solacing of a needy world; the joy of being able to distinguish the first faint outlines of the Plan, and the subsequent even greater joy of subscribing some small share towards its realisation.

Yes, the spiritual life should be full of joy, and joy should be the keynote of the aspirant; the joy engendered by the Soul will make its presence felt even during periods of profound personality distress and unhappiness. Joy lets in the Light, dispels glamour and misunderstanding, and evokes strength for the task that lies ahead. Joy in the recognition of inner strength leads to the undertaking of tasks which previously seemed insuperable, and ensures successful accomplishment. Joyfulness therefore becomes the hallmark of the server.

4

PLANES OF EXISTENCE

The theme to be set out below is founded on the Ancient Wisdom teachings, which the ordinary person might regard as rather far-fetched and mainly theoretic, because these concepts in their beauty and impressiveness range way beyond all normal human conception. In fact, with these mental ventures man can at best merely touch the outer fringes of Reality. A schematic framework can be devised to provide a general outline of the principles involved, but this will only represent a vague image, because the limited human mind can envisage no true picture of the several supernal but ephemeral states of being. Man is only able to recognise a minute and insignificant part of the total physical manifestation of Creation, so how can he expect to form even an approximate picture of the higher and more ethereal realms of existence? All that really matters is that man should come to the realisation that the conditions he is experiencing in his present life on Earth are merely serving him as an elementary introduction to an infinite existence of so much vaster, more imposing and exalted proportions.

But back to Earth, meanwhile still allowing our imagination the freest possible scope.

For the average person there is only one plane of conscious existence, and that is the physical which can be discerned by his five senses. When his attention is drawn to it, he will, however, realise that as far as his feelings are concerned, he is largely functioning on the plane ruled by his emotions, that is the *emotional* or *astral plane*. In addition he is probably becoming aware that he is also operating in a sphere connected with his thought-life, and which may be distinguished as the *mental plane*. There are relatively only few who have actually attained *spiritual levels,* because even many of the religious minded apparently have not yet raised their consciousness beyond the astral levels, as their religion still largely remains emotionally focused, only occasionally perhaps touching the mental plane. Instances where the religious life is sufficiently profound to life the individual to spiritual spheres, must be regarded as exceptional.

Yes, the plane of existence reached by the individual on his endless evolutionary path, remains purely a question of consciousness. Although physical, emotional and mental progress are contributory factors, the decisive point is how these factors have influenced the consciousness. It is therefore the degree of consciousness attained by the Soul, that will determine the plane on which it will be functioning at any particular stage of its development.

As is the case with so many other aspects of creation, the planes of existence are also founded on a septenary system. First of all there are the *Seven Cosmic Planes*:

I   The *Cosmic* Divine Plane
II   The *Cosmic* Monadic Plane
III The *Cosmic* Spiritual Plane
IV The *Cosmic* Intuitional Plane
V   The *Cosmic* Mental Plane
VI The *Cosmic* Astral Plane
VII The *Cosmic* Physical Plane

Each of these seven Planes, which range totally beyond man's comprehension, are again subdivided into seven subsidiary planes. It is, however, only the lowest of these supernal planes, the Cosmic Physical, which directly or consciously concerns our Solar System, and includes:

1. The *Systemic* Divine Plane
2. The *Systemic* Monadic Plane
3. The *Systemic* Spiritual Plane
4. The *Systemic* Intuitional Plane
5. The *Systemic* Mental Plane
6. The *Systemic* Astral Plane
7. The *Systemic* Physical Plane

These are the seven planes in which the human being finds his existence. Of these planes the majority of individuals are only consciously aware of life on the lowest or physical level, with an awakening and expanding awareness of the surrounding astral and mental planes.

For the sake of interest it can be mentioned that each of the Systemic Planes are again subdivided into a further seven planes. Thus the *Systemic Physical Plane* is classified into:

(a) The First Etheric or Atomic Plane
(b) The Second Etheric or Sub-atomic Plane
(c) The Third Etheric or super-Etheric Plane
(d) The Fourth Etheric or Etheric Plane
(e) The Gaseous Plane
(f) The Liquid Plane
(g) The Dense Physical Plane

In subsequent chapters it will be pointed out that the souls of the majority of men on Earth, after "death" of the physical vehicle, will temporarily depart from the material world to take up their abode for a longer or shorter period in one of the seven astral spheres. The actual level to which he will be assigned will depend on the nature of the life that was led while in the flesh and on the corresponding degree of consciousness developed. But more about this will follow.

During incarnation the astral spheres are hidden from the material world by an *etheric web* which forms an impenetrable barrier to the normal physical senses. It is only under exceptional circumstances, when man succeeds in raising his consciousness to certain required levels, that he is enabled to penetrate this dividing etheric web and to enter and become acquainted with new worlds of being. In due course the advancing pilgrim will however find that such escape from limiting confines, is only a relative concept, because as soon as he has adjusted himself to his new environment, he will discover that he is again restricted by fresh boundaries of consciousness, the surmounting of which will form his next objective.

5

THE LAW OF CAUSE AND EFFECT

KARMA

As has already been stressed *"All is Energy"*. Furthermore, every form of manifestation has its own etheric surround, not only serving as the medium of reception and radiation of all energies relating to the body concerned, but simultaneously linking it with every adjoining form whatever its nature. This joining and merging of one etheric body with the next, means that an etheric complex is in existence which serves to synthesize every single form of creation, whether an atom, a man or celestial body, into one single etheric world or universe, one co-ordinated whole, the ONE.

This etheric web, reticulated down to atom levels, but at the same time embracing all the heavens and outer space, therefore acts as a linking medium whereby energies or forces are transmitted from point to point, or from source to destination. Owing to this fantastic framework, this close coherence and interrelation between every form of creation it is, however, hardly possible to refer to either a single source or a single destination of energy. To what extent pristine energy emanates from the One Primordial Source, lies beyond human conception, but as far as man's understanding can determine, each and every change occurring within our system or environment is the outcome of the perpetual inflow of *seven* major *Rays of Energy* from outer space. Each of these Rays is characterised by its own specific qualities, having either a positive or negative effect upon the phenomenal form with which it comes into contact, as determined by various circumstances.

As far as the present approach is concerned, however, it is only intended to stress the fact that as a result of these constantly moving streams of energy, conducted through the vital and interwoven etheric surround, every form of manifestation remains subject to a perpetual state of impact by both external and internal influences, bringing about a never ending process of change and adaptation. These changes are always present and actively functioning whether discernable to human senses or not.

What is both so interesting and important, however, is that every single change in each and every body of manifestation, will inevitably also have some effect on neighbouring bodies, because all these forms are intimately connected and therefore interrelated by the etheric web through which energy vibrations are carried from form to form. These vibrations are actually relayed into the greater and infinite etheric reservoir, but the distance at which their effect will remain distinguishable before they fade out, will depend on their potency at the point of origin. All this is founded on the basic principle that *every action leads to a corresponding reaction*, but that such response becomes progressively more diffused as it is dispersed further from its source.

The only logical conclusion that can be arrived at is that every form of change, whether large or small, and whether considered important or negligible, is produced by some cause or energy impact, and must inevitably result in some or other effect. Such effect will, however, in turn be reflected in the etheric surround, causing a fresh vibration and consequently also a new range of causes, the strength of which will be in direct proportion to the "cause-effect" inducing this vibration, and which will now become the cause of further effects on surrounding bodies. The effectiveness or rate at which the potency of the cause-effect decreases will depend on circumstances and the extent to which the respective energy can be successfully directed and retained in a reasonably concentrated form, or whether it is allowed to diffuse into the etheric surround.

And thus our whole system and the whole Universe is compounded of a continuous, most intricate and never ending series of interdependent and closely interacting and integrated causes and effects, which in their totality constitute our ever evolving system, which man recognises as Life.

These general considerations are the fundamental principles underlying the *Law of Cause and Effect*, more commonly known as "*Karma*".

Every form of manifestation is constantly subject to the Law of Karma, but apart from its general application it remains of particular interest to the individual human being, because it so intimately affects his whole existence – his past, the present and his whole future. It must be stressed, however, that apart from individual karma, regarded from the narrower and purely personal point of view, there are also the broader aspects of karma, such as Cosmic, World, National, Group and Family Karma, which may often play an unrealised but nevertheless a relatively important role in determining the individual destiny. Whereas man can do a great deal towards directing the nature, course and effect of his personal karma, he usually stands helpless with regard to the greater issues which he will simply have to accept, merely being a negligible pawn in the vaster game of life.

The deeper implications of the Law of Karma, with its many ramifications, are far beyond the comprehension of man. In the form life of our planet there lie hidden certain divine causes affecting the course of life, which are apparently founded on basic principles which are far above the mental reach of any human being. Causes and effects which can be recognised as such by the mind, must therefore be regarded as only of a secondary nature. On the other hand this is the only form of karma that falls within man's intelligent reach, and which he therefore has any hope of controlling once some reasonable understanding of the principles concerned is achieved.

As far as individual karma is concerned, it should be realised that this is the product of forces originating from the mind and subsequently finding expression as thoughts, words and deeds, having their effect on the personality itself, on fellow men, and on the immediate environment. The cumulative effect of such expression is, however, not only related to the present and future, because that which is experienced today, reflecting the present state of our minds, is largely the result of thoughts, attitudes and activities of the past. This past again does not only refer to preceding days, weeks or years of the present life, but also represents the cumulative effect of unredeemed activities from previous existences.

Regarded separately, many of these thoughts and activities may seem of a fleeting nature and of negligible importance, but nonetheless "thoughts are things" and although apparently trivial and insignificant, they remain part of our subjective being and obedient to the laws of nature, and must inevitably leave some trace or effects. These issues steadily accrue in man's etheric surround, taking on ever more pronounced proportions, which at some stage or other simply must have some influence on the current and future life of the individual. In which direction such accumulating forces will gravitate, whether they will have a positive or negative effect, or whether they will incline towards the good or bad, will entirely depend on the nature and quality of the dominating thought complex. In this connection it should be noted that when causes are due to ignorance and consequent lack of thought, there is less responsibility and karmic results will not be so severe. It is when activities are deliberately motivated by lust and desire, by material greed and selfishness, that some form of retribution becomes unavoidable.

As might be expected karmic processes are closely associated with the laws of reincarnation and the course of evolution. During the early evolutionary stages, and while lives are still dominated by the lower urges of the personality, and the purer influences of the Soul do not yet seem to leave any adequate impression, a heavy mass of dark karma is steadily being accumulated, which at some phase of man's future development will have to be effaced by so-called misfortunes, by afflictions or the many other trials of life. It is only as incarnation succeeds incarnation, with the Soul influence gradually gaining supremacy over the material bodies of expression, that the accrued karmic debts of the past will step by step be eliminated. This will be an indication that the human atom is progressively disassociating and freeing itself from the imposed lower influences of the personality, with a simultaneous closer association and recognition of the higher impulses of the Soul while steadily gaining control over its vehicles of expression.

Meanwhile there are, however, also the influences of group and other forms of world karma which the individual can never escape, and which will remain the final controlling factor determining his eventual destiny. He will nevertheless always remain responsible for the course of events within the narrower precincts of his personal endeavour.

These thoughts automatically lead to the question of *Free Will*. Because the individual constitutes but an insignificant part of humanity, and is of even less consequence in the greater world of being, he is bound to be engulfed and swept hither and thither by forces far beyond his trivial control. Meanwhile, however, he still remains in command of his own free will, by means of which he can regulate and utilize energy and forces which concern his own direct circumstances and physical, emotional and mental environment. The extent and direction in which this free will is applied while discriminating and choosing between various pairs of opposites, will in the first instance determine the immediate course of events as far as such an individual is concerned, *but*, and this must be emphasized, always subject firstly to his personal karma, and secondly also to several forms of more comprehensive world karma.

During the course of each Soul's development, the stage will fortunately be reached eventually when he will awaken to the recognition of the Law of Cause and Effect. This in fact means reaching the phase when the will and purpose of the Soul, the Inner Being, will begin to manifest itself, indicating the turning point in the evolutionary life, when the footsteps will be redirected towards the Path of Return. This is the stage when a purposeful beginning will be made in neutralising the accrued store of negative karma, and the systematic building of positive karma. The workings of karma will then be recognised and become apparent in events and happenings which otherwise would have been inexplicable, and might have been regarded as unjust and undeserved manifestations of fate. Such recognition will require a certain degree of understanding of the underlying principles, which will then also result in a new approach to life, moving away from the purely emotional reactions, and developing the conscious awareness that there must be some valid reason for each and every occurrence which happens to come our way, affecting not only our present state of being, but also the future.

Such awareness of the karmic role of both thoughts and actions, must inevitably have a most decisive influence with regard to the individual's attitude towards the adversities of life, with a growing realisation that he is directly responsible for the building of either the good or bad aspects of his personal karma, and that he can thus largely contribute toward the shaping of his own future destiny.

In this connection St. Paul has also aptly stated that: "A man reaps what he sows. If he sows seed in the field of his lower nature, he will reap from it a harvest of corruption, but if he sows in the field of the Spirit, the Spirit will bring him a harvest of eternal life. So let us never tire of doing good, for if we do not slacken our effects we shall in due time reap our harvest. Therefore as opportunity offers let us work for the good of all". (Gal. 6:7–10)

The Law of Cause and Effect is sometimes referred to as the Law of Retribution, but this expression is inclined to leave an entirely wrong impression. It is largely because man's attitude towards life during the past has been mainly negative and the product of wrong impulses and of selfish desire, that he has steadily been accumulating a heavy load of bad karma. This in turn has been responsible for the inclination to associate karma only with unpleasant conditions. The Law of Karma is, however, entirely unbiased, and its positive or negative effects will solely be the result of existing energies or negative effects will solely be the result of existing energies and conditions, which means a reflection of the truism that "energy follows thought".

The effects of thoughts, words and actions will therefore be purely in accordance with the underlying motivation. Should these elements, responsible for the direction of energy, be wrongly inspired and therefore of a corresponding evil nature, then the bad karma will ensue, which at some stage or other, either in the present or some future life, will have to be equated. On the other hand, depending on the motivations, thought and activities, there could be as much good as bad karma, and by a changed attitude towards life, focussing the available energies on such tenets as love, understanding and altruism, mainly good karma could be engendered, ensuring a future that will be characterised by the inner joy realised by fulfilling the higher objectives of the Soul.

In this connection it is perhaps just as well to remember that whereas evil in the first instance emanates from the material aspects of the personality, good karma originates from the spiritual qualities of the Soul which is progressively gaining ascendance over the lower nature. Although there are larger issues which range beyond man's control, there are many other aspects which concern his daily life, where it is his privilege to apply his free will. It is by the discerning and discriminative use of this prerogative that the individual can contribute so much towards adjusting and transcending evil karma. It should furthermore be regarded as one of the responsibilities of each person whose eyes have been opened by a deeper understanding of the verities of life, to share such knowledge with his fellow men, thereby unfailingly also adding to his store of good karma. As may be expected the neglect of such opportunities will have exactly the opposite effect.

The Soul is being reincarnated from life to life in order to gain experience in the material worlds, and thus to learn and evolve. A relatively placid and uneventful existence would therefore in many respects amount to a wasting of time, because such a life would present but few opportunities for spiritual progress. An existence crowded with adventure of a pleasant nature will as a rule be welcomed, but will yield relatively little of a positive nature. The most valuable lessons are provided by life's many afflictions and trials. It is the overcoming of such adversities that will eventually ensure satisfactory growth. But how many are there who will honestly be prepared to welcome life's misfortunes and scourges in order to be granted these advantages? No, to the contrary, as the wheels of fortune proceed over life's bumpy way, harassed cries of distress are far more likely to be heard, attended by complaints that these reverses are undeserved.

Once the aspirant begins to realise, however, that his troubles are not due to the manipulations of some capricious destiny, or the harsh punishment meted out by a vengeful God, but that his miseries are in fact merely the result of certain laws of nature taking their course, and that his adversities are largely of his own making and of a karmic nature, then this will be a clear indication that he has reached one of the most vital milestones of his existence.

One of the notable features of the Law of Cause and Effect, which should always be kept in mind, is that the result of past errors can also be neutralised or at lease be qualified to a considerable extent by a new and more favourable approach to the present circumstances of life. It lies within man's own hands to liquidate the mistakes committed in the past, and bad karma can be changed and commuted in accordance with the extent of the will-to-good. What a pity therefore if the negative aspects of karma are over-accentuated, leaving the individual in a state of acquiescence and fear, and with a lack of will to overcome the effects of past transgressions. By purposeful, intelligent and loving direction of the forces of good, these must and will inevitably nullify and triumph over that which is evil and harmful. The effectiveness of such helpful and healing energies can also be relied upon. By becoming aware of the conflict of these opposing forces, by relinquishing every form of selfishness, and superseding these with the forces of goodwill and right human relations, the success of the spiritual forces will be assured and the benefits of such an attitude will rapidly become apparent. Man is thus to a large extent responsible for his own heaven or hell, both here and hereafter.

6

MAN'S SPIRITUAL EVOLUTION

It was under the sway of the Law of Cause and Effect that spirit and matter were blended to become manifested as material creation, serving as an additional channel for the diverse and vital expressions of Life on our planet Earth. Though cyclic and rhythmic repetition related groups of forms periodically made their appearance, only to fade out again and to be replaced in due course by forms attuned to a somewhat higher vibration. And thus life gradually advanced through aeons of time, at first through the elemental or involutionary stages, subsequently to be followed by various phases in the three lower kingdoms of nature, and eventually to be superseded in part by life in the human kingdom.

These four lower kingdoms, however, merely represent consecutive and transient stages in the never-ending evolutionary cycle, which will finally be culminated by life in the spiritual kingdoms.

As far as the human being as such is concerned, a clear distinction should be drawn between the evolutionary process in the three worlds of the personality. These phases refer to physical, emotional and mental spheres of existence, which are jointly merely serving as vehicles of expression for the soul, the subjective entity who is meanwhile slowly but surely evolving towards its own destination.

The spiritual development in man can essentially be regarded as a struggle for dominance between the opposites of matter and spirit, or between the lower vehicles of expression and the indwelling Soul. Through a growing discrimination the latter is being enabled to distinguish between darkness and light, between the unreal and the real. As far as the individual is concerned, there is an increasing awareness of the presence of the Inner Being and a gradual recognition that this silent Inner Guide is in fact the true Self, responsible for that insistent voice of conscience whose precepts can always be relied upon.

The evolutionary urge of the human being, that irresistible impulse to push forward along the Lighted Way "from darkness into light, from the unreal to the real, and from death to immortality", is a divine attribute inherent in all created forms and for which the human mind can give no satisfactory explanation.

The life of the evolving entity may be divided into five progressive steps, which are determined by the condition of the indwelling spiritual flame and the quality of the light that is being radiated.

It should be realised, however, that although these stages are here only sketchily indicated in a few paragraphs, their sequence actually covers innumerable incarnations, spread over vast periods of time which may be reckoned in terms of millions of years; Especially during the early stages of existence, man's development is extremely slow, and it is only when nearing his culmination and when the Soul is beginning to take hold, that a marked increase in the rate of unfoldment will occur.

Furthermore, students should realise that the classification as set out below, is artificial and is merely given to provide an overall picture of the general process of development. The procedure will in fact vary considerable from soul to soul, both in rate and characteristics, and in some instances the periods described might partly overlap or even show a somewhat simultaneous development.

The *First Period* – the recognition of man as a human being dates from that prehistoric time when animal-man was provided with an individual soul, and thus gained 'self'-consciousness – he was 'individualised'. In this early stage man was still polarised partly in his physical body and was learning to control it by means of the desire or emotional body. This corresponds with the ancient historical periods of Lemuria and Atlantis. During this period man as yet had no knowledge or awareness of any higher existence, and his aspirations did not go beyond pandering to the lusts and pleasures of the flesh.

This period may be compared with that of a child between the ages of one and seven years.

46

At this stage the inner flame of the soul is as yet hardly noticeable to the Teachers of the race, and only appears as a small pinpoint of light, the driving force of evolution still largely remaining instinctive.

The *Second Period* is characterised by a polarisation in the emotional body, and is associated with the first signs of an awakening lower mind of desire. This occurred during the later Atlantean days. With the mind beginning to permeate the personality, the desires no longer remain solely focused on the physical life, but become directed towards the astral level, and a capacity arises for a deep love and unreasoning devotion for those exhibiting greater intelligence and wisdom, or in wild and unreasonable hatred towards some associates. The balance which the reasoning mind will later achieve is, however, still lacking and the life during this period will therefore be characterised by emotional extremes. The mental aspect is unfolding, but the man is still dominated by the emotions.

If this period is symbolically compared with that of a single life, it will correspond with the life of a child of seven to fourteen years old – the period covering adolescence and the maturing of the child.

The inner light of the Soul remains dim during this stage, and will hardly be noticeable.

The *Third Period* is that vital phase when the mind is being developed, and the life is polarised in the mental body.

The man by now has full control of the physical body, and each incarnation provides better equipment, with the accent primarily on the quality of the brain as the instrument of the mind. Simultaneously the emotional body becomes more refined in its life of desire, and instead of as in the past turning downwards to the material for its satisfaction, it now tends upwards, and desire becomes transmuted into aspiration – at first mental aspiration, until later there comes an awareness of the existence of the subjective worlds. The man also becomes conscious of the joys of the intellect, and therefore ever strives for greater adequacy of the mind.

Meanwhile the divine spark of the soul, which for so long has remained dormant, has commenced to glow and to develop into a small flame. This spiritual fire is permeating the contents of the Soul, supplying it with warmth, radiating its energies, and allowing the soul to gain in consciousness on its own plane. The physical brain, however, does not yet become consciously aware of impressions issuing from this indwelling force.

This period will correspond with the individual age of between fourteen and twenty – the reaching of adulthood.

The *Fourth Period* is that wherein the Personality, as a co-ordinated whole, if for the first time being recognised – the three lower bodies, the physical, emotional and mental, have become synthesized into a single working unit under mental control. The consummation of the personality life has been attained and its attention is now being consciously focused towards the Soul.

This is the stage where the aspirant is born, and where he takes his first hesitant steps on the Path. He has become aware of his duality; he comes to the realisation that his whole being will finally have to become centred in the Soul, and that the Soul must come into complete control of the lower planes. He therefore commences to work on this transmutation and the expansion of his consciousness; he finds this a laborious and painful task, marked by constant reverses and which can only be achieved by dedication and persistence. He finds that his most effective tools for this demanding task are study, meditation and service to his fellow man.

In the course of these struggles, and without the aspirant being aware of it, his inner fire has systematically been provided with more fuel and is now burning so much brighter, that the inner light is beginning to attract the attention of the Masters.

This marks the maturing adult stage of twenty-eight to thirty-five years.

The *Fifth Period* denotes the consummation of the human being on the physical plane. It is the stage where he enters the Path of Initiation – initiation into the conscious recognition of the spiritual worlds.

Through sustained meditation, supported by its two help-meets, study and service, the aspirant is increasingly making direct contact with the Soul's vibration, and more and more the soul-consciousness is being incorporated to include the lower planes. The Soul light is burning ever brighter, and its radiation is lighting up the disciple's Path.

During this period the focus is being shifted entirely from the Personality to the Soul, until towards the end of the fifth stage liberation is complete and the man is set free. The next step is that the polarisation shifts even higher, to become centred in the Spiritual Triad, but this only occurs after the Third Initiation has been attained.

The fifth period may be compared with the symbolic age of forty-two.

It is often found that workers become impatient or discouraged with their slow spiritual progress, but it should always be remembered that all truly esoteric effects are slowly achieved, and that only after consistent and painstaking work. Should a man make apparently rapid progress in any one incarnation, this will be due to the fact that he is only recapitulating that which was already acquired in earlier incarnations, and that he is preparing for his next arduous task.

The whole path of spiritual evolution is therefore a successive range of expansions of consciousness, of recognitions and succeeding revelations, until the world of matter and form stands revealed in the light of the Soul, and illumination is achieved. The aspirant then gradually establishes his conscious life in the subjective world, the world of reality; his sense of values becomes radically changed and his time and capacities are devoted to higher objectives.

THE AURA

As pointed out above, spiritual unfoldment is a slow and laborious progress, during which the vibrations of the Inner Being are gradually increased and steadily raised to ever-higher levels. It is characterised by the rhythmic building of inner structures, until a phase is reached when these are found lacking and are broken down to be superseded by new ideas. Over the ages this course is systematically proceeding, with the focus of the personality life slowly shifting in accent, at first from the physical to the emotional, and subsequently to mental and intuitional levels. These changes will unavoidably entail phases of intense distress and perplexity, of inner struggle and conflict with both fellow men and environing conditions, bringing severe pain and agony to all concerned.

All this misery is caused by the extremely difficult process of constant purification and adaptation which the lower bodies have to experience. Old rhythms come into conflict with new, resulting in the sudden or gradual elimination of temporary systems which have served their purpose. Such new vibrations will, however, hardly become stabilised before the whole construction will again be subjected to renewed change while the process is being recapitulated, but each time probably on a somewhat higher vibration.

During the course of innumerable re-incarnations, each of the lower bodies will thus successively, and step by step, be disciplined, purified, readjusted, reconstructed, mutually adapted, and induced to react to higher vibrations, finally to be brought under domination of the Soul, and thus to serve as instruments of experience.

As the physical body is purified and refined, and the emotional and mental surrounds are raised to higher levels, their rate of vibration will also be consistently increased, which to the clairvoyant will be clearly reflected in the colour of the surrounding etheric body or *aura*. This colour of the aura by which every person is surrounded and qualified, will also allow Our Friends from subjective levels to gauge at a single glance the state of spiritual development attained by any individual. The vibrations emanating from primitive man are slow and sluggish, resulting in a murky aura, whilst those radiated from the more advanced individual are considerably higher, producing a clear and bright aura, which in the highly developed should literally become a shining light, radiating his inner illumination to all and sundry.

CONSCIOUSNESS

Expansion of consciousness is generally speaking synonymous with and a clear indication of spiritual development. It is an indication that the Soul is gradually asserting itself by discarding the limitations of the three lower worlds. This means that the imprisoned Soul is progressively gaining its freedom, and with the clearer light thus generated, the mind is provided with ever increasing consciousness.

On the other hand a relatively advanced state of evolution may sometimes be achieved without the individual being consciously aware of his raised subjective status, or of his true spiritual gifts and capacities. These will, however, unfailingly be brought to expression when the need arises and when these assets can be applied to public benefit.

The capacity of expanding the human consciousness seems practically unlimited, although this will mean that when the highest forms of consciousness are achieved, embracing those of the spiritual realities, the material bodies of the human kingdom will finally have to be relinquished in favour of the better suited ethereal conditions of the spiritual spheres.

One of the most effective ways of liberating the consciousness is by applying available capacities to the benefit of fellow men. Through selfless service the imprisoned consciousness will systematically be released, provided such service is rendered intelligently, with intuitive understanding and is inspired by a spirit of love.

GLAMOUR AND ILLUSION

Because the bulk of mankind is still emotionally inclined, it remains subject not only to world glamour but also to self-induced personal glamour. The fogs of the astral plane distort the vision of the aspirant and provide him with a false picture of all that he is concerned with, thus also preventing him from obtaining a clear concept of his environment and of the realities of life. Although the gratification of physical and emotional desire may provide shorter or longer periods of pleasure and happiness, this will remain of a temporary nature because founded on deceptive astral values. Such periods will consequently only be succeeded again by trouble and distress.

For life after life the average person has mainly been conditioned by the many distortions of glamour. For the greater part of his existence he has been dominated by the various phases of desire, until with the progress of time such desire has gradually begun to be transmuted into aspiration leading to a realisation of the deeper verities of life. It is only when this stage is achieved that it slowly dawns on the mind to what extent the past has been governed by glamour, and also the appalling nature of these glamours, which with all their misrepresentations and misunderstandings, were responsible for former regrettable thoughts, attitudes and activities.

For the dissipation of glamour it is first of all essential that its presence should be recognised by the light of the mind, which will eventually lead to progressive revelation of ever new aspects of Truth and Reality, and therefore to fresh expansions of consciousness and the growing Light of the Soul.

During the later phases of spiritual evolution some of the major impediments often encountered consist of various forms of glamour and illusion.

Illusion is the plight experienced by the Soul during the early stages of its awakening, when the mind and brain are still partly obscured owing to lack of illumination. This consequently leads to misinterpretations and distortions of thought-forms and ideas. When such mental illusion is further aggravated on the astral plane by intense desire or emotion, it is referred to as glamour.

The problem of illusion can to a large extent be overcome by meditation and by gaining reasonable control of the mind in order to develop the intuition, which is the only effective instrument for the dispelling of illusion.

INITIATION

When after endless struggles the aspirant gains a certain degree of conscious light, then his further advance along the Path of Return may for the sake of clearer understanding be beaconed off into what are known as "Initiations".

These initiations merely serve to indicate progressive stages of advance along the Way, each successive initiation marking the ever brighter burning of the Inner Flame, resulting in a purer conception of, and a closer integration with all that lives. This in turn will result in constantly expanding horizons, widening fields of activity and service, and correspondingly increasing responsibility. It will also lead to clearer vision and consciousness, and consequently to a growing awareness of the Divine Plan and of that small fraction of the Plan which will directly concern the relative aspirant.

Once the 'stream of initiation' has been entered, temporary delays and deviations are bound to occur during the course of the extended process, which will be stretched over the sequence of many lives. But there will be no turning back, and the individual will steadily be swept onwards to the House of the Father.

During this sustained development the aspirant will learn to distinguish ever more clearly between good and evil; he will learn to recognise the transient nature of the material world, and that these values must eventually be sacrificed in favour of that which is spiritual. This will finally eventuate in his liberation. It is only by gaining freedom from physical and astral fetters that deeper and more comprehensive Wisdom will be achieved, which in due course will in turn be commuted to true Intuition. With the entering of these successive states of consciousness and the opening up of new horizons before the initiate's expanding vision, the hidden mysteries of our Solar System will sequentially be revealed to the exploring mind.

The explorer must, however, be prepared for the fact that as he advances from stage to stage to ever higher planes of thought and activity, and in order to attain the necessary freedom required to enter the next plane and the new fields of experience, he will voluntarily have to sacrifice all that to which he had become accustomed and attached, and which may even have become dear to his heart.

It is important that the student should gain a reasonable understanding of the processes which concern his spiritual unfoldment and therefore also of the fundamental principles of initiation. That is should become his ideal to achieve ever higher steps of initiation is admirable, provided that such striving is correctly motivated. Should there be the least suspicion that such aims are animated by a disposition to achieve a higher status or wield more power, then the aspirant is exposing himself to evil influences and is definitely looking for trouble. No, there should be only one inducement, and that is to become a more efficient instrument in the hands of those Guiding Entities who serve the interests of humanity or the Divine Plan in general.

It should be realised that initiates are merely serving as the links for the transmission of thoughts, energies and the wishes of those operating on spiritual levels to the human and other kingdoms of nature still confined to mater. Each initiate, according to the circumstances and position he occupies, must therefore be regarded as a light bearer to bring some or other form of illumination to his surroundings.

There are seven recognised initiations in human development, but as is the case with all else, as soon as it concerns the higher or spiritual aspects, the average man can to some extent consider or ponder on these matters, but actually they largely transcend his understanding. A reasonable conception of the nature of the lower initiations which lie within reach of the earnest striver can, however, still be achieved:

FIRST INITIATION (The Birth of the Initiate)

The Soul, after innumerable reincarnations in order to gain experience in the material worlds, during the course of ages eventually evolves to the stage where at long last the Path of Return can be entered. In the human being this phase is indicated when man, after becoming aware of the presence of higher objectives, begins to assume a somewhat revised attitude towards the purely physical and emotional demands of the personality. This is reflected by a growing yearning for that which is more exalted, with a corresponding resistance and aversion to the persistent claims of the flesh.

For practical purposes it may be regarded that the First Initiation has been attained when the Soul has gained reasonable control over the three aspects of the lower vehicle. This will be denoted when various forms of desire are no longer allowed full sway, and such excesses as gluttony, drinking and sensuality are brought somewhat under control. It is the stage when pure selfishness is gradually being suppressed, to be superseded by greater consideration and kindliness towards fellow men; when emotional feelings such as hate, envy, spite and jealousy are systemically being replaced by goodwill and loving understanding; when the gap between the lower and higher minds is gradually being bridged, and when contact is slowly being established with the subjective worlds.

As may be expected, during the early phases the aspirant will often fail in realising his higher objectives by succumbing to the temptations of the flesh. So this process is slow, will entail constant struggle and will be characterised by continual suffering, misery and distress. This conflict with the lower bodies will as a rule be spread over several lives before a reasonable degree of mastery is achieved.

This development will not conform to any fixed sequence of procedure, but will differ according to the circumstances, karma and nature of each individual, with the main objective of accomplishing the difficult task of disciplining and subduing the many forms of long established desire.

It is only reasonable to expect that periodic lapses in accomplishing these difficult attempts at changing the ingrained patterns of life will occur, but what really matters is that the aspirant should display the courage, persistence and determination eventually to overcome his lower inclinations. It is the inner motivation that is of importance, and whether the aspirant is inspired, probably still unconsciously, by the inner Christ-consciousness.

Today there are thousands in every country of the world who already have attained their First Initiation, either in the present or some previous life. The majority of these aspirants are as yet quite unaware that this status in their development has been achieved, but those who watch from beyond the veil will realise the true position and will lend their valuable support to allow these novices to get their feet firmly established on the newly entered Path of Initiation.

A characteristic of this phase of development is that the aspirant is becoming aware of the duality of his existence, because with recurring frequency he is confronted with the inner struggle between the Soul and the Personality, and the many ensuing alternatives between which he has to decide.

SECOND INITIATION (The Baptism)

Probably one of the most difficult conflicts over which the aspirant will have to prevail, is the mastering of the emotional nature, or in other words, the gaining of reasonable control over the astral body. It is the attaining of this victory by the Soul that marks the entry into the second phase of initiation.

One of the surest indications that the Soul is gaining dominance over the emotional life, is that the mind is consistently being illuminated by the Soul, and this consequently leads towards the gradual dissipation of the many astral glamours, thus allowing clearer discernment of the realities of being. This will furthermore result in ever broadening fields of activity, especially with regard to the serving of humanity. This urge to serve, to understand and to express goodwill to all, will also steadily lead to further rapid unfoldment, and may even eventuate in attaining the Third Initiation in the same life in which the Second Initiation was realised.

THIRD INITIATION (The Transfiguration)

Our Friends on the 'other side' regard the first two Initiations which have been briefly dealt with above, as merely preliminary and preparatory to the Third Initiation, which, according to them, should be considered as the First Major or Spiritual Initiation. It is at this stage that the aspirant really becomes 'transfigured' and consciously enters the Spiritual Kingdom.

Whereas with the previous two introductory Initiations command has been achieved over the physical and emotional spheres of existence, the Soul is now also gaining mastery over the mental vehicle, which means that for the first time the Soul will be in complete control of all three aspects of the Personality. The Soul and Personality are thus becoming integrated into a single unit, which henceforth will be able to function as a Soul-infused being. For the individual this will signify a complete 'transfiguration', a consummation of life's highest objectives and for the Soul it will denote liberation from the many restrictions of the personality, and recognised admittance as a junior member into the ranks of the Hierarchy of Spiritual Beings.

The Soul will now be able to serve consciously and therefore with greater efficiency not only as a link but also as an adequate channel for the interchange of energy between the Hierarchy and the lower Kingdoms. With this transfiguration the entire Soul-infused personality becomes directly illumined with the Light emanating from the Monad or Spirit, which is now enabled to pour its divine energies into this newly prepared channel. The integrated personality thus becomes an exclusive instrument of the Soul, serving the Spiritual Kingdom as another point of anchorage in the world of matter for consciously transmitting the supernal energies into the three worlds of human endeavour.

With the reaching of this stage, the consciousness is also completely liberated and can now freely function either in or out of the form to conform with the requirements of the Plan. The initiate can now at will, and with the retention of full consciousness, enter the higher spheres, temporarily leaving the lower worlds far behind. With the merging of the material and spiritual aspects they have become completely at-one, opening the way for the even more supernal union with the Monad, which will finally lead to definite emancipation from the three worlds. The 'way of escape' of the soul now becomes its 'way of daily living', with all forms of pain steadily being transcended. This of course also applies to all other emotional qualities, such as every form of both suffering and pleasure, of bitterness, misery and torment. All these will from now on be superseded by the joy of perpetually serving the Powers of Light!

FOURTH INITIATION (The Renunciation)

With the Fourth Initiation the initiate is at last brought face to face with his own Monad, his 'Father in Heaven', who so far as only been known as the spiritual Entity inspiring the Soul. As a result of this direct contact between the Monad and the Soul-infused personality, the functions of that vague concept, the Soul, which for aeons has served as the intermediary between the Monad and its instrument of manifestation in the three lower worlds, now becomes redundant. The Soul is consequently absorbed within the Monad and disappears as a separate entity, and in its place nothing is left but the energy of Love-Wisdom, and the dynamic Divine Will as directed by the Monad.

The Fourth Initiate therefore is directly controlled by his Monad, by means of what might be called a 'Bridge of Light'. For as long as the initiate has to function or appear in the three worlds of men, he avails himself of a 'personality' which to the average man will have a perfectly normal appearance. The form side of existence is, however, at this stage no longer needed as a medium for gaining experience, from now on it will only serve as an outer mask through which the initiate or the Master may unobtrusively work among men to fulfil some spiritual purpose. This personality or body of expression will therefore not be the product of physical procreation, but will be *Self-created* by the Will and Purpose of the Monad, and it will thus not be subject to the normal laws of nature.

This body of manifestation will not in any way limit the initiate or hold him prisoner; by means of the applied will it can at any time and according to the requirements of circumstances be 'dissolved' or made to fade away from human vision; it can be radically changed in outer appearance, or can be transferred at a moment's notice from one part of the world to another.

With the Great Renunciation everything that used to shackle the aspirant to the material world is relinquished in order that the energies and powers which the initiate controls may be applied to the benefit of mankind as a whole. He is now dominated by the energy of the will-to-good. He is still aware of the experiences gleaned from his numerous physical incarnations, but he has discarded all that proved insignificant, retaining only the essence which has to be transmuted into wisdom. As the purified distillation of the past, his destiny now faces new realms of experience and spiritual ventures, which will lead him from human evolution to Spiritual Evolution and ultimately to the choice of one of the Seven Cosmic Paths.

FIFTH INITIATION (Revelation)

According to human standards man has attained perfection when he is ready for the Fifth Initiation. This also marks the time when the Initiate has gained sufficient wisdom, love and spirituality to be admitted to the acknowledged ranks of the Masters of Wisdom.

The Initiation of Revelation will place in the initiate's hands the power to wield Light as the carrier of Life to all in the three worlds. To his vision will also be revealed the next step to be taken upon the Way of Higher Evolution. The Way is then revealed to him in a totally new light, and it therefore signifies the true emergence of the initiate from the tomb of darkness of material being, and the entrance into the world of Reality and of Spiritual Being which lies beyond all that man has hitherto sensed or known.

What is reflected here are merely the personal interpretations of the Tibetan's teachings. Realms of thought and existence are being dealt with which are as yet far beyond the conception of the ordinary human being and are only briefly expressed to round off the picture which has so far been sketched. It is realised that to the unimaginative man in the street these thoughts may represent just ludicrous nonsense, or at best the whimsical fantasies of a fanciful dreamer!

HIGHER EVOLUTION (The Seven Cosmic Paths)

As already pointed out, the Path of Evolution is never ending. When from the human standpoint liberation has been achieved after the Fifth Initiation, new realms of expansion will be revealed to the initiate. The realms to be trodden will ultimately include the whole cosmic sphere, and are divided into Seven Cosmic Paths of Evolution, each Path being determined by one of the Seven Cosmic Rays of Energy.

Each initiate has the free decision to follow whichever Path he chooses, but the probability is that as a result of the Law of Attraction, the initiate's choice will be strongly influenced by his vibration as induced by his Monadic Ray. Some of these Paths may keep the initiate linked to the Hierarchy and to Earth service for many aeons to come, whilst others may lead to wider planetary activities within our Solar System, or else to outer-planetary or cosmic activities. The final decision as to the Path to be followed must be made at the consummation of the *Sixth Initiation* the *Initiation of Decision*. From this decision there will apparently be no turning back.

To conclude with it should be noted that the entire mental and spiritual evolutionary process of man is founded on the theme of impression and subsequent revelation. This impression of thoughts and ideas emanates from Spiritual Spheres, and is a process that has been proceeding consistently over the ages, with man only rarely being consciously aware of the supernal help he is receiving, and of the endless patience with which this support is being imparted.

Once the aspirant awakens to the fact of the presence of and the assistance available from these higher Entities, he can however be developed into a far more effective instrument for recognising and conveying ever new revelations and forms of knowledge to be used on behalf of his fellow men. It should, however, always be remembered that such awakening and subsequent growth will only be attained through experience and sustained hard work.

And thus during the course of ages, and under the guidance of Superior Being directing divine Energies, and after experiencing innumerable reincarnations, man's instinct has been transmuted into intellect, and subsequently this intellect will gradually be commuted to intuition. Slowly but surely man will become aware of his divine potentialities and destiny. This inner divinity will systematically be unfolded, raising primitive man to attain the most superior heights of human existence. This development will bring forth the many ideas, inspirations and revelations characterising the present widespread and advanced techniques and scientific developments on every terrain, the capacity for the creation and appreciation of art and beauty in its many forms, all contributing to spiritual enrichment.

Meanwhile, however, man still remains a dual-being, a combination of spirit and matter, of good and evil, with the forces of selfishness, hate and desire being opposed to and contending with the powers of love, altruism, understanding and goodwill. Although it may take time and unrelenting patience and persistence, man may however rest assured that the powers for good will finally supervene, leading to a world in which spiritual values will strike the keynote and will clearly be brought to expression by improved human relationships at all levels.

These developments are steadily leading to a climax which will culminate in the awareness that the Kingdom of God can actually function within the bounds of human activity on Earth. This Kingdom is however something that must be earned individually by each person; it is a condition which, to begin with, will only be manifested immanently, but which can notwithstanding be experienced and appreciated even though the surroundings may be in a state of material or emotional chaos.

7

THE HIERARCHY OF MASTERS OF WISDOM

A cursory outline has already been sketched of the systematic evolution of man from the primitive savage, until the state of the initiate has finally been attained. This evolution is actually of a dual nature. On the one hand there is that of the perishable physical vehicle with its supplementary surrounds, which ensures the survival of the race by sexual reproduction, and the transmission of acquired attributes from generation to generation by means of chromosomes contained within the reproductive cells. At the same time there is, however, also the immanent spiritual being, the Soul, representing the immortal aspect and which evacuates the material body when a span of life is terminated at "death".

After release from its physical bonds the Soul, depending on its stage of development, passes over to an appropriate subjective sphere. In the course of time, and after a longer or shorter sojourn in the etheric worlds, which will be determined by the needs of each particular Soul, the urge for further experience in the world of matter will develop and the Soul will be reincarnated into a new young body for renewed trials and adventures in the world of form.

The real individual, the immortal Self, is therefore not the transient and perishable personality, but the indwelling Soul. When the Soul after aeons of time and innumerable incarnations has evolved to what is known as the Third Initiation, the stage is reached where it gains final dominance over the lower bodies of the personality. This indicates the stage when the Soul has achieved liberation, with no further need to return to the three lower worlds of experience. This is also the stage when the initiate enters the Kingdom of God by becoming consciously aware of the spiritual worlds, where he will be acknowledged and accepted as a junior member in the ranks of the Hierarchy of Masters of Wisdom. It is, however, only after attaining the Fifth Initiation that he will be able to assume the responsibilities of a full-fledged Master.

THE NATURE OF THE SPIRITUAL HIERARCHY

The Hierarchy of Masters constitutes an assembly of Supernal Beings whose function it is to serve in an executive capacity for promoting the divine evolutionary objectives of the Entity manifesting through our planet Earth. These Beings serve as intermediaries between the even more exalted divine planetary forces and the human and lower kingdoms, with the purpose of advancing human and lower kingdoms, with the purpose of advancing human self-consciousness, as well as raising the consciousness of the animal, vegetable and mineral kingdoms of nature.

After having triumphed over matter, these Elder Brothers of humanity have raised themselves during the course of ages from the ranks of ordinary human beings. This means that during their development they have treaded the same paths, have endured the same struggles and suffered the same ordeals as those humanity is still being subjected to today. They are consequently eminently qualified to lead and guide their younger brothers still bound in matter and with their vision obscured and distorted by the astral spheres.

Our Friends are characterised by an enduring *Love* for all that lives, by an inexhaustible source of *Knowledge* that can readily be amplified at will or need, and which through the all pervading energy of love, has been transmuted into *Understanding* and *Wisdom*.

The Hierarchy resorts under the control of the Lord of the world, supported by a Trinity, with the Christ functioning as the World Teacher, and in charge of that aspect of the Hierarchy which is concerned with human development. It must be kept in mind, however, that apart from the human evolution there also exist the closely related parallel evolutions of the other kingdoms of nature, each of which also demands hierarchical support.

This group of "Supermen" represents the forces of intelligence which guide the development of our Earth. Their expanded consciousness provides the channel for the expression of the Energy which might be called the Will of God for the realisation or manifestation of the Divine Plan. They are the instruments of planetary evolution and are aware of the exact stage of human attainment, and of the next steps which have to be taken. These Supernal Beings are thus also the teachers of those who still have to struggle through the miasma of material existence. For this purpose they avail themselves of the intellect of the more advanced individuals, whose minds they impress with appropriate thoughts and ideas for further dissemination amongst their fellow men.

The Hierarchy stands for freedom and for the liberty of individuals, groups or races, allowing them to advance along the Path of Light, each according to his circumstances, specific qualities and the opportunities with which he may be provided. This is effective through the Love aspect of the Divine Purpose. Members are responsible for the wielding, directing and controlling of the energies required for activating the Law of Evolution. They avail themselves of the desires, aspirations and thoughts of men at various levels of development, to turn and focus these forces into creative activity for the promotion of human progress.

The Hierarchy is the custodian of that part of the Divine Purpose which esoterically is known as the *Divine Plan*, and is associated with the evolutionary development of Humanity. Such details of the plan which are intended for immediate accomplishment, are telepathically impressed on the minds of those workers and servers in the ranks of men who are able to bring them to expression as creative thought, ideas and ideals. Men are thus used as instruments for the manifestation of the relative aspects of the Plan.

The Energy of Love is dispersed by the Hierarchy through the many initiates, at various degrees of development, and found throughout the world and in all nations. These men are the idealists and servers striving towards increased Light and the upliftment of their fellow men, and who are expressing the inflowing love-wisdom energy by introducing the principles of brotherhood, fellowship, co-operation, goodwill and better understanding, thus bringing about gradual improvement in human relationships. These workers are often misunderstood, because they are not interested in sentimental and emotional love of purely personal nature, but are mainly interested in promoting the broader principles of love that will affect larger groups or communities. Their love is frequently expressed by their efforts towards the more liberal and equitable sharing of the many benefits which life so bountifully bestows on man. They do not primarily concern themselves with the trifling affairs of the individual, but rather the matters of a more comprehensive nature which affect mankind as a whole.

One of the principal objectives of the Hierarchy is therefore to discover and contact those with the necessary sensitivity and perception who can register the truths and revelations which it is intended to convey, and which will subsequently be formulated and transmitted with a minimum of distortion. It is important that these basic revelations should be expressed as simply as possible. The imparting of knowledge by the Masters to their disciples is effected by telepathically impressing receptive minds.

All intercourse within the Hierarchy is also effected by telepathic communication and impression between mind and mind, because the spoken word is only manifested on lower levels of existence where physical organs are available for their expression.

Some of the specific functions of the Hierarchy may perhaps be briefly summarised. As far as mankind will permit, the Masters direct world events but always taking care not to infringe unduly on human *free-will*. Their influence is conveyed by impressing or implanting certain ideas and providing revelations which will affect the tide of human affairs. The Hierarchy also serves as a wall of protection between humanity and many forms of excess evil. Some of these evil forces emanate from cosmic sources, and with their extreme potency would already have proved disastrous to human existence if it had not been for the active protection and counter measures provided on the part of the Masters.

The Hierarchy prepares their human disciples for initiation not only by stimulating them with an inflow of energies originating from the Lord of the World, but also by providing suitable opportunities for service with regard to the unfolding Divine Plan. In this respect special attention is also accorded to humanity in an effort at awakening and increasing the consciousness aspect of all forms in each of the kingdoms of nature.

Although there are individuals who may to some extent recognise the importance of the many functions which the Hierarchy fulfils in guiding the destiny of men, only those already well advanced along the Path can form a clearer concept of the wide scope of their activities in the invisible worlds.

It should be remembered that like all else in the world of creation the constitution of the Hierarchy also remains subject to constant change and evolution. There is an uninterrupted inflow of aspiring disciples who are qualifying for adoption as junior members into the lower ranks of this eminent organisation, whilst at the same time certain Masters are equipping themselves for major initiations, and are thus being prepared to be raised to even more exalted spheres of activity. These new fields of experience may still be within our planetary system, but might also imply assuming the duties of some cosmic nature. What must be stressed however, is that each individual soul or entity, whatever his status or destiny, remains on the evolutionary path and is steadily unfolding to ever higher forms of consciousness, entailing ever increasing responsibilities.

These changes are not, however, limited to the individual members, but are also reflected in the Hierarchy as a whole, as this system is also constantly adjusting itself to perpetually changing conditions and to new demands and functions.

The eventual destiny of the Hierarchy is to become more closely associated with humanity. This will be accomplished under the leadership of the Christ. When in due course, and stimulated by the Energy of Love, this more intimate synthesis has been established, the Christ, representing both Humanity and the Hierarchy, will, through the Energy of Wisdom, relate these two planetary centres to the Lord of the World, thus allowing the unrestrained inflow of divine energy from supernal spheres. The imminent reappearance of the Christ on Earth, when he will again freely associate with man and take part in human affairs, will also pave the way for the progressive return and externalisation of large numbers of the Masters of Wisdom. This will not only be to promote the interests of Humanity, but it should be remembered that there is also a simultaneous spiritual unfoldment of the Hierarchy itself, and this closer association with Humanity must be regarded as an essential step in the destiny of hierarchical development. The Hierarchy itself has reached a point of spiritual crisis, and its members are being impelled towards this reincarnation on the physical plane and a consequent life of practical service to man, by higher forces which are also controlling their future in conformance with the unfolding Divine Plan and Purpose.

Because the Masters have been liberated from all restrictions of the lower worlds of matter, they have also been exempted from all pain and suffering associated with matter and form life. They have now become dedicated to the task of uplifting the lower kingdoms of nature and of serving Humanity by assisting their younger brothers towards achieving greater spiritual freedom.

Although liberated from the three worlds of human experience, a Master can by act of the will mentally create and appropriate a physical body whenever this may be needed as an instrument of service. Such a *"body of manifestation"* can be either created or dissolved instantaneously, and may assume any specific outer appearance in accordance with requirements. As a rule this created body will be rebuilt closely to resemble the original physical body in which the Master took his last initiation while still on Earth. To the average person this body of manifestation will appear to be perfectly normal, thus enabling the master to move about unrecognised in any human society while engaged on his particular mission.

8

BETTER UNDERSTANDING OF "DEATH"

The existing general fear of death and also the intense grief and unhappiness so often caused by the loss of loved ones, is largely due to man's ignorance concerning his own state of being and the natural laws of existence, as well as his lack of knowledge concerning the nature and meaning of death and of what may be expected in the after-life.

Deeper insight into the laws governing both human life and death, and more especially a clearer discernment of what happens to the spirit after departing from the physical body and passing beyond the obscuring veil, should therefore help considerably towards dispelling the fear of death and of the hereafter. Furthermore, such better understanding and the knowledge that this break is not final, as the loved ones continue to exist in the subjective realms with retention of full consciousness, should contribute towards relieving the pain of survivors who suddenly have to take leave of someone who has been near and dear to them. Moreover there also remains the prospect of future reunion.

In the foregoing chapters an attempt has been made to provide a brief survey of man's Path through Life, with the hope that this might serve as a general framework into which the experiences to be recorded in the following pages may be fitted. It is considered that such a background may also tend towards a somewhat better understanding by the uninformed, who suddenly may be confronted with phases of existence of which in the past they were totally unaware, or which so far remained an enigma to them owing to lack of knowledge in respect of these matters.

No attempts are being made to prove the existence of an after-life. This is a premise of which every unbiased thinker who has made a fair study of this subject, will remain convinced. The problem which requires greater clarification, however, is the actual nature of this hereafter, and also what the individual may expect to encounter when passing over. It is this aspect which is not always properly understood and on which it is hoped to throw some clearer light.

A great deal of evidence about the after-life has become available over the years, and some interesting instances of this will be set out in the following chapters.

The problem nevertheless remains that while man continues to be limited by his physical vehicle, and his observations and experiences are dependent on his five senses, it is apparently impossible for him to form a true picture of the more ephemeral conditions ruling in the subjective worlds. It seems furthermore that no amount of explanation will enable us really to understand those conditions where other dimensions and laws of nature are brought into play. In addition our outlook remains clouded and distorted by the astral sphere by which each and every normal human being is surrounded. As each individual is responsible for the construction of his own particular astral surround, which will differ from that of all others, each individual will be prone to his own peculiar illusion, and will view and interpret any specific set of conditions and circumstances in his own way, thus arriving at his own conclusions which might actually differ widely from those of his neighbours.

It therefore stands to reason that details of what has been experienced in the subjective worlds will vary to some extent, because each being will observe conditions in these spheres in accordance with his specific character and his own particular state of development. And because no two individuals are identical in every respect, it may therefore also be expected that the afterlife will be viewed from different points of reference, each from his own level of discernment and understanding. Only after man has liberated himself from the limitations of his astral fetters, and has moved into the brighter light of the higher realms, will he be able to discern more clearly and arrive at a better understanding of the true nature of these subjective spheres.

9

BIBLICAL PERSPECTIVES

Texts derived from the "GOOD NEWS BIBLE"

The Bible is probably largely the product of inspired writings by enlightened spiritual leaders of past centuries. The quality of such writings depend to a considerable extent on the purity and integrity of the physical instrument through which it is expressed. Except in some rare instances, it is only to be expected that such messages are affected to greater or lesser extent by the minds of the respective channels, resulting in larger or smaller distortions of the relative teachings.

After all these centuries the attributes of the recipients of these teachings, and the prevailing conditions under which they were received, can no longer be determined, and their reliability can consequently not be established beyond all doubt. Under the circumstances it is only reasonable that every statement in the Bible cannot be accepted at its face value by the unprejudiced student, merely on the grounds that it has been included in this outstanding collection of religious teachings by a group of fallible human beings. In addition many of the accounts are symbolical, or have been set out in the form of parables, and must consequently be studied as such, often leaving a relatively wide sphere for individual interpretation or conjecture.

Furthermore, many of the subjects being dealt with, especially those concerning the higher spiritual worlds, quite often range far beyond normal human understanding, and are consequently also frequently couched in terms hiding or camouflaging their true meaning. Care should therefore be taken not to be too dogmatic with the interpretation of some of these biblical texts. It is this uncertainty about the construction to be attached to certain statements, that has largely been responsible for much of the religious controversy of the past, as well as for the hundreds of sects, denominations and schools of thought which characterise the Christian religion.

Notwithstanding the above limitations, and the fact that these teachings were in the first instance intended for the relatively undeveloped people and conditions of many centuries ago, the basic principles of human behaviour, of mutual relationships, and of spiritual precepts, remain unaltered, and with certain reservations the Bible must still be considered as one of the valuable sources for esoteric study. Considered in conjunction with later esoteric writings, it will be found that the bible contains many deeper verities of which the casual reader, unacquainted with the Ancient Wisdom teachings, remains blissfully unaware.

On the whole the Bible, however, provides surprisingly frugal information about the conscious after existence, and of what may be expected in the augured heavenly life.

At first glance some of the passages quoted may seem to have no evident bearing on the main theme of this book. Quiet reflection on the subject will as a rule, however, reveal some aspects of direct or indirect relationship. At any rate it was felt that they belonged!

1. LIFE AND DEATH

1 COR. 15:20–55 Life after Death

Christ has been raised from death, as the guarantee that those who sleep in death will also be raised. ... The last enemy to be defeated will be death. ...

Someone will ask, "How can the dead be raised to life? What kind of body will they have?"

... There are heavenly bodies and earthly bodies; the beauty that belongs to heavenly bodies is different from the beauty that belongs to earthly bodies. ...

This is how it will be when the dead are raised to life. When the body is buried, it is mortal; when raised, it will be immortal. When buried, it is ugly and weak; when raised, it will be beautiful and strong. When buried, it is a physical body; when raised, it will be a spiritual body. There is, of course, a physical body, so there has to be a spiritual body. For the scripture says, "The first man, Adam, was created a living being"; but the last Adam is the life-giving Spirit. It is not the spiritual that comes first, but the physical, and then the spiritual. The first Adam, made of earth, came from the earth; the second Adam came from heaven. Those who belong to the earth are like the one who was made of earth; those who are of heaven are like the one who came from heaven. Just as we wear the likeness of the man made of earth, so we will wear the likeness of the Man from Heaven.

What I mean, brothers, is that what is made of flesh and blood cannot share in God's Kingdom, and what is mortal cannot possess immortality.

Listen to this secret truth: we shall not all die, but when the last trumpet sounds, we shall all be changed in an instant, as quickly as the blinking of an eye. For when the trumpet sounds, the dead will be raised, never to die again, and we shall all be changed. For what is mortal must be changed into what is immortal; what will die must be changed into what cannot die. So when this takes place, and the mortal has been changed into the immortal, then the scripture will come true: "Death is destroyed; victory is complete!"

"Where, Death is your victory?
Where, Death is your power to hurt?"

ROM. 6:1–11 Eternal Life in Union with Christ

Just as sin is ruled by means of death, so also God's grace rules by means of righteousness, leading us to eternal life through Jesus Christ our Lord.

... We have died to sin – how then can we go on living in it? For surely you know that when we were baptized into union with Christ Jesus, we were baptized into union with his death. By our baptism, then, we were buried with him and shared his death, in order that, just as Christ was raised from death by the glorious power of the Father, so also we might live a new life.

For since we have become one with him in dying as he did, in the same way we have become one with him by being raised to life as he was. And we know that our old being has been put to death with Christ on his cross, in order that the power of the sinful self might be destroyed, so that we should no longer be the slaves of sin. For when a person dies, he is set free from the power of sin. Since we have died with Christ, we believe that we will also live with him. For we know that Christ has been raised from death and will never die again – death will no longer rule over him; and now he lives his life in fellowship with God. In the same way you are to think of yourselves as dead, so far as sin is concerned, but living in fellowship with God through Christ Jesus.

ROM. 7:6 The Way of the Spirit

(With the death of the physical body) ... No longer do we serve in the old way of a written law, but in the new way of the Spirit.

1 JN. 3:14 Love Brings Eternal Life

We know that we have left death and come over into life; we know it because we love our brothers. Whoever does not love is still under the power of death.

LK. 2:34–38 Rising from Death

Jesus answered them, "The men and women of this (physical) age marry, but the men and women who are worthy to rise from death and live in the (Spiritual) age to come will not then marry. They will be like angels and cannot die. They are the sons of God, because they have risen from death. And Moses clearly proves that the dead are raised to life. In the passage about the burning bush he speaks of the Lord as the God of Abraham, the God of Isaac, and the God of Jacob! He is the God of the living, not of the dead, for to him all are alive."

DAN. 12:1–3 The Time of the End

The angel wearing linen clothes said, "At the time the great angel Michael, who guards your people, will appear. Then there will be a time of troubles, the worst since nations first came into existence. When the time comes, all the people of your nation whose names are written in God's book will be saved. Many of those who have already died will live again: some will enjoy *eternal life*, and some will suffer *eternal disgrace*. The wise leaders will shine with all the brightness of the sky. And those who have taught many people to do what is right will shine like the stars for ever."

JN. 11:25–26 Perpetual Life

Jesus said to her, "I am the resurrection and the life. Whoever believes in me will live, even though he dies; and whoever lives and believes in me will never die."

1 THES. 4:13–17 The Lord's Coming

Our brothers, we want you to know the truth about those who have died, so that you will not be sad, as are those who have no hope. We believe that Jesus died and rose again, and so we believe that God will take back with Jesus those who have died believing in him.

What we are teaching you now is the Lord's teaching: we who are alive on the day the Lord comes will not go ahead of those who have died. There will be the shout of command, the archangel's voice, the sound of God's trumpet, and the Lord himself will come down from heaven. Those who have died believing in Christ will rise to life first; then we who are living at that time will be gathered up along with them in the clouds to meet the Lord in the air. And so we will always be with the Lord.

2. DARKNESS AND LIGHT

JN. 1:2–5 The Word

From the very beginning the Word was with God. Through him God made all things; not one thing in all creation was made without him. The Word was the source of life, and this life brought light to mankind. The light shines in the darkness, and the darkness has never put it out.

JN. 3:19–21 Loving the Darkness

The light has come into the world, but people love the darkness rather than the light, because their deeds are evil. Anyone who does evil things hates the light and will not come to the light, because he does not want his evil deeds to be shown up. But whoever does what is true comes to the light in order that the light may show that what he did was in obedience to God.

JN. 12:35–36 People of the Light

Jesus answered, "The light will be among you a little longer. Continue on your way while you have the light, so that the darkness will not come upon you; for the one who walks in the dark does not know where he is going. Believe in the light, then, while you have it, so that you will be the people of the light. … (46) I have come into the world as light, so that everyone who believes in me should not remain in darkness."

EPH. 5:8–14 The Light Reveals

You yourselves used to be in the darkness, but since you have become the Lord's people, you are in the light. So you must live like people who belong to the light, for it is the light that brings a rich harvest of every kind of goodness, righteousness, and truth. Try to learn what pleases the Lord. Have nothing to do with the worthless things that people do, things that belong to the darkness. … Anything that is clearly revealed becomes light.

1 JN. 1:5–7 God is Light

God is light, and there is no darkness at all in him. If, then, we say that we have fellowship with him, yet at the same time live in the darkness, we are lying both in our words and in our actions. But if we live in the light – just as he is in the light – then we have fellowship with one another, and the blood of Jesus, his Son, purifies us from every sin.

1 JN. 2:9–10 Living in the Light

Whoever says that he is in the light, yet hates his brother, is in the darkness to this very hour. Whoever loves his brother lives in the light.

3. JUDGEMENT AND PUNISHMENT

JN. 12:44–50 Judgment

Jesus said in a loud voice, "Whoever believes in me believes not only in me but also in him who sent me. Whoever sees me sees also him who sent me. I have come into the world as light, so that everyone who believes in me should not remain in the darkness. If anyone hears my message and does not obey it, I will not judge him. I came, not to judge the world, but to save it. Whoever rejects me and does not accept my message has one who will judge him. The words I have spoken will be his judge on the last day! This is true, because I have not spoken on my own authority, but the Father who has sent me has commanded me what I must say and speak. And I know that his command brings *eternal life*. What I say, then, is what the Father has told me to say."

MT. 25:31–46 The Final Judgment

When the Son of Man comes as King and all the angels with him, he will sit on his royal throne, and the people of all the nations will be gathered before him. Then he will divide them into two groups, just as a shepherd separates the sheep from the goats. He will put the righteous people on his right and the others on his left. Then the

King will say to the people on his right, 'Come you that are blessed by my Father! Come and posses the kingdom which has been prepared for you ever since the creation of the world. I was hungry and you fed me, thirsty and you gave me a drink; I was a stranger and you received me in your homes, naked and you clothed me; I was sick and you took care of me, in prison and you visited me.'

The righteous will then answer him, 'When, Lord, did we ever see you hungry and feed you, or thirsty and give you a drink? When did we ever see you a stranger and welcome you in our homes, or naked and clothe you? When did we ever see you sick or in prison, and visit you? The King will reply, 'I tell you, whenever you did this for one of the least important of these brothers of mine, you did it for me!'

Then he will say to those on his left, 'Away from me, you that are under God's curse! Away to the *eternal fire* which has been prepared for the Devil and his angels! I was hungry but you would not feed me, thirsty but you would not give me to drink; I was a stranger but you would not welcome me in your home, naked but you would not clothe me; I was sick and in prison but you would not take care of me.'

Then they will answer him, 'When, Lord, did we ever see you hungry or thirsty or a stranger or naked or sick or in prison, and would not help you?' The King will reply, 'I tell you, whenever you refused to help one of these least important ones, you refused to help me.' These, then, will be sent off to *eternal punishment*, but the righteous will go to eternal life.'

ZEPH. 1:17–18 The Day of Judgment

The Lord says, "I will bring such disasters on mankind that everyone will grope about like a blind man. They have sinned against me, and now their blood will be poured out like water, and their dead bodies will lie rotting on the ground."

On the day when the Lord shows his fury, not even all their silver and gold will save them. The whole earth will be destroyed by the fire of his anger. He will put an end – a sudden end – to everyone who lives on earth.

JN. 3:36

Whoever believes in the Son has eternal life; whoever disobeys the Son will not have life, but will remain under God's punishment.

ROM. 1:18–20 God's Anger

God's anger is revealed from heaven against all the sin and evil of the people whose evil ways prevent the truth from being known. God punishes them, because what can be known about God is plain to them, for God himself made it plain.

ROM. 2:3–11 God's Judgment

Do you think you will escape God's judgment? Or perhaps you despise his great kindness, tolerance, and patience. Surely you know that God is kind, because he is trying to lead you to repent. But you have a hard and stubborn heart, and so you are making your own punishment even greater on the Day when God's anger and righteous judgments will be revealed. For God will reward every person according to what he has done. Some people keep on doing good, and seek glory, honour, and immortal life; to them God will give eternal life. Other people are selfish and reject what is right, in order to follow what is wrong; on them God will pour out his anger and fury. There will be suffering and pain for all those who do what is evil, for the Jews first and also for the Gentiles. But God will give glory, honour, and peace to all who do what is good, to the Jews first, and also to the Gentiles. For God judges everyone by the same standard.

4. THE DEVIL

REV. 12:7–9 War in Heaven

Then war broke out in heaven. Michael and his angels fought against the dragon, who fought back with his angels; but the dragon was defeated, and he and his angels were not allowed to sty in heaven any longer. The huge dragon was thrown out – that ancient serpent, called the Devil or Satan, that deceived the whole world. He was thrown down to earth, and all his angels with him.

MT. 12:2–28 Driving Out Demons

Jesus said … "Any country … town or family that divides itself into groups which fight each other will fall apart. So if one group is fighting another in Satan's kingdom, this means that it is already divided into groups and will soon fall apart! You say that I drive out demons because Beelzebul gives me the power to do so. … No, it is not Beelzebul, but God's Spirit, who gives me the power to drive out demons."

EPH. 6:10–16 The Armour of God

Build up your strength in union with the Lord and by means of his mighty power. Put on all the armour that God gives you, so that you will be able to stand up against the Devil's evil tricks. For we are not fighting against human beings but against the wicked spiritual forces in the heavenly world, the rulers, authorities, and cosmic powers of the dark age. So put on God's armour now! Then when the evil day comes, you will be able to resist the enemy's attacks; and after fighting to the end, you will still hold your ground.

So stand ready, with truth as a belt tight round your waist, with righteousness as your breastplate, and as your shoes the readiness to announce the Good News of peace. At all times carry faith as a shield; for with it you will be able to put out all the burning arrows shot by the Evil One.

1 PET. 5:8–10 Your Enemy, the Devil

Be alert, be on the watch! Your enemy, the Devil, roams round like a roaring lion, looking for someone to devour. Be firm in your faith and resist him, because you know that your fellow-believers in all the world are going through the same kind of sufferings. But after you have suffered for a little while, the God of all grace, who calls you to share his eternal glory in union with Christ, will himself protect you and give you firmness, strength and a sure foundation.

1 JN. 3:7:8 Belonging to the Devil

Let no one deceive you, my children! Whoever does what is right is righteous, just as Christ is righteous. Whoever continues to sin belongs to the Devil, because the Devil has sinned from the very beginning. The Son of God appeared for this very reason, to destroy what the Devil has done.

REV. 20:1–3 The Thousand Years

Then I saw an angel coming down from heaven, holding in his hand the key of the abyss and a heavy chain. He seized the dragon, that ancient serpent – that is, the Devil, or Satan – and chained him up for a thousand years. The angel threw him into the abyss, locked it, and sealed it, so that he could not deceive the nations any more until the thousand years were over. After that he must be left loose for a little while.

2 THES. 2:4–10 The Wicked One

The Wicked One will even go in and sit down in God's Temple and claim to be God.

... the wicked One will be revealed, but when the Lord Jesus comes, he will kill him with the breath from his mouth and destroy him with his dazzling presence. The Wicket One will come with the power of Satan and perform all kinds of false miracles and wonders, and use very kind of wicked deceit on those who will perish. They will perish because they did not welcome and love the truth so as to be saved.

5. HELL

MT. 5:27–30 Committing Adultery

You have heard that it was said, 'Do not commit adultery.' But now I tell you: anyone who looks at a woman and wants to possess her is guilty of committing adultery with her in his heart. So if your right eye causes you to sin, take it out and throw it away! It is much better for you to lose a part of your body than to have your whole body thrown into hell. If your right hand causes you to sin, cut it off and throw it away! It is much better for you to lose one of your limbs than for your whole body to go to hell.

MT. 10:28 Fear God

Do not be afraid of those who kill the body but cannot kill the soul; rather be afraid of God, who can destroy both body and soul in hell.

LK. 12:5 Fear God, who, after killing, has the authority to throw into hell. Believe me, he is the one you must fear!

JAS. 3:6 The Evil Tongue

The tongue is like a fire. It is a world of wrong, occupying its place in our bodies and spreading evil through our whole being. It sets on fire the entire course of our existence with the fire that comes to it from hell itself.

2 PET. 2:4–10 Punishment

God did not spare the angels who sinned, but threw them into hell, where they are kept chained in darkness, waiting for the Day of Judgment. God did not spare the ancient world, but brought the flood on the world of godless people …

The Lord knows how to rescue godly people from their trials and how to keep the wicked under punishment for the Day of Judgment.

LK. 16:22–25 Hades

The poor man died and was carried by the angels to sit beside Abraham at the feast in heaven. The rich man died and was buried, and in Hades, where he was in great pain, he looked up and saw Abraham, far away, with Lazarus at his side. So he called out, 'Father Abraham'. Take pity on me, and send Lazarus to dip his finger in some water and cool my tongue, because I am in great pain in this fire!'

But Abraham said, 'Remember, my son, that in your lifetime you were given all the good things, while Lazarus got all the bad things. But now he is enjoying himself here, while you are in pain.'

6. ANGELS – Messengers and Agent of God

GEN 21:15–19 Hagar and Ishmael Are Sent Away

When the water was all gone, she (Hagar) left the child under a bush and sat down about a hundred metres away. She said to herself, "I can't bear to see my child die." While she was sitting there, she began to cry.

God hear the boy crying, and from heaven the angel of God spoke to Hagar, "What are you troubled about, Hagar? Don't be afraid. God has heard the boy crying. Get up, and pick him up, and comfort him. I will make a great nation out of his descendants." Then God opened her eyes, and she saw a well. She went and filled the leather bag with water and gave some to the boy.

GEN. 28:12–13 Jacob's Dream at Bethel

(Jacob) dreamt that he saw a stairway reaching from earth to heaven, with angels going up and coming down on it. And there was the Lord standing beside him. "I am the Lord, the God of Abraham and Isaac," he said. "I will give to you and to your descendants this land on which you are lying."

NUM. 22:31–33 Balaam and his Donkey

Then the Lord let Balaam see the angel standing there with his sword; and Balaam threw himself face downwards on the ground. The angel demanded, "Why have you beaten your donkey three times like this? I have come to bar your way, because you should not be making this journey. But your donkey saw me and turned aside three times. If it hadn't, I would have killed you and spared the donkey."

1 KGS. 19:5–9 Elijah on Mount Sinai

(Elijah) lay down under the tree and fell asleep. Suddenly an angel touched him and said, "Wake up and eat." He looked round, and saw a loaf of bread and a jar of water near his head. He ate and drank, and lay down again. The Lord's angel returned and woke him up a second time, saying, "Get up and eat, or the journey will be too much for you." Elijah got up, ate and drank, and the food gave him enough strength to walk forty days to Sinai, the holy mountain. There he went into a cave to spend the night.

PS. 103:19–21 Praise the Lord

The Lord placed his throne in heaven;
    he is King over all.
Praise the Lord, all you heavenly powers,
    you servants of his, who do his will!
Praise the Lord, all his creatures
    in all the places he rules.
Praise the Lord, my soul!

MT. 13:36–43 Jesus Explains the Parable of the Weeds

"Tell us what the parable about the weeds in the field means."

Jesus answered, "The man who sowed the good seed is the Son of Man; the field is the world; the good seed is the people who belong to the Kingdom; the weeds are the people who belong to the Evil One; and the enemy who sowed the weeds is the Devil. The harvest is the end of the age, and the harvest workers are angels. Just as the weeds are gathered up and burnt in the fire, so the same thing will happen at the end of the age; the Son of Man will send out his angels to gather up out of his Kingdom all those who cause people to sin and all others who do evil things, and they will throw them into the fiery furnace, where they will cry and grind their teeth. Then God's people will shine like the sun in their Father's Kingdom."

MT. 24:31 The Coming of the Son of Man

The great trumpet will sound, and he will send out his angels to the four corners of the earth, and they will gather his chosen people from one end of the world to the other.

MT. 28:1–3 The Resurrection

Mary Magdalene and the other Mary went to look at the tomb. Suddenly there was a violent earthquake; an angel of the Lord came down from heaven, rolled the stone away, and sat on it. His appearance was like lightning, and his clothes were white as snow.

LK. 1:11–19 The Birth of John the Baptist is Announced

An angel of the Lord appeared to him, standing on the right of the altar where the incense was burnt. When Zechariah saw him, he was alarmed and felt afraid. But the angel said to him, "Don't be afraid, Zechariah! God has heard your prayer, and your wife Elizabeth will bear you a son (John)."

… Zechariah said to the angel, "How shall I know if this is so? I am an old man, and my wife is old also."

"I am Gabriel," the angel answered. "I stand in the presence of God, who sent me to speak to you and tell you this good news."

L. 1:26–31 The Birth of Jesus is Announced

In the sixth month of Elizabeth's pregnancy God sent the angel Gabriel to a town in Galilee name Nazareth. He had a message for a girl promised in marriage to a man named Joseph, who was a descendant of King David. The girl's name was Mary. The angel came to her and said, "Peace be with you! The Lord is with you and has greatly blessed you!"

Mary was greatly troubled by the angel's message, and she wondered what his words meant. The angel said to her, "Don't be afraid, Mary; God has been gracious to you. You will become pregnant and give birth to a son, and you will name him Jesus …"

LK. 2:8–15 The Shepherds and the Angels

There were some shepherds in that part of the country who were spending the night in the fields, taking care of their flocks. An angel of the Lord appeared to them, and the glory of the Lord shone over them. They were terribly afraid, but the angel said to them, "Don't be afraid! I am here with good news for you, which will bring great joy to all the people. This very day in David's town your saviour was born – Christ the Lord! And this is what will prove it to you: you will find a baby wrapped in strips of cloth and lying in a manager."

Suddenly a great army of heaven's angels appeared with the angel, singing praises to God:

"Glory to God in the highest heaven,
and peace on earth to those with
whom he is pleased!"

when the angels went away from them back into heaven, the shepherds said to one another, "Let's go to Bethlehem and see this thing that has happened, which the Lord has told us."

GUARDIAN ANGELS

PS. 34:7

His angel guards those who obey the Lord
and rescues them from danger.

PS. 35:4–6

May those who plot against me
be turned back and confused!
May they be like straw blown by the wind
as the angel of the Lord pursues them!
May their path be dark and slippery
while the angel of the Lord strikes them down!

PS. 91:11–12

God will put his angels in charge of you
to protect you wherever you go.
They will hold you up with their hands
to keep you from hurting your feet on the stones.

DAN. 6:21–22 Daniel in the Pit of the Lions

Daniel answered, "God sent his angel to shut the mouths of the lions so that they would not hurt me. He did this because he knew that I was innocent and because I have not wronged you."

EX. 23:20–23 Guiding Angel

"I will send an angel ahead of you to protect you as you travel and to bring you to the place which I have prepared. Pay attention to him and obey him. Do not rebel against him, for I have sent him, and he will not pardon such rebellion. But if you obey him and do everything I command, I will fight against all your enemies. My angel will go ahead of you and take you into the land of the Amorites, … and I will destroy them."

IS. 37:36 Destroying Angels

An angel of the Lord went to the Assyrian camp and killed 185,000 soldiers. At dawn the next day there they lay, all dead!

JUDG. 13:2–21 The Birth of Samson

At that time there was a man named Manoah from the town of Zorah. He was a member of the tribe of Dan. His wife had never been able to have children. The Lord's angel appeared to her and said, "You have never been able to have children, but you will soon be pregnant and have a son. Take care not to drink any wine or beer, or eat any forbidden food; and after your son is born, you must never cut his hair, because from the day of his birth he will be dedicated to God as a Nazirite. He will begin the work of rescuing Israel from the Philistines."

Then the woman went and said to her husband, "A man of God has come to me, and he looked as frightening as the angel of God. I didn't ask him where he came from, and he didn't tell me his name. But he did tell me that I would become pregnant and have a son. He told me not to drink any wine or beer, or eat any forbidden food, because the boy is to be dedicated to God as a Nazirite as long as he lives."

Then Manoah prayed to the Lord, "Please, Lord, let the man of God that you sent come back to us and tell us what we must do with the boy when he is born."

God did what Manoah asked, and his angel came back to the woman while she was sitting in the fields. Her husband Manoah was not with her, so she ran at once and said to him, "Look! The man who came to me the other day has appeared to me again."

Manoah got up and followed his wife. He went to the man and asked, "Are you the man who was talking to my wife?"

"Yes", he answered.

Then Manoah asked, "When your words come true, what must the boy do? What kind of a life must he lead?"

The angel answered, "Your wife must be sure to do everything that I have told her. She must not eat anything that comes from the grapevine; she must not drink any wine or beer, or eat any forbidden food. She must do everything that I have told her."

Manoah did not know that it was the Lord's angel, so he said to him, "Please do not go yet. Let us cook a young goat for you."

But the angel said, "If I do stay, I will not eat your food. But if you want to prepare it, burn it as an offering to the Lord."

Manoah replied, "Tell us your name, so that we can honour you when your words come true."

The angel asked, "Why do you want to know my name? It is a name of wonder."

So Manoah took a young goat and some grain, and offered them on the rock altar to the Lord who works wonders. While the flames were going up from the altar, Manoah and his wife saw the Lord's angel go up towards heaven in the flames. Manoah realised then that the man had been the Lord's angel, and he and his wife threw themselves face downwards on the ground. They never saw the again...

The woman gave birth to a son and named him Samson.

ACTS 5:18–21 The Apostles are Persecuted

They arrested the apostles and put them in the public jail. But that night an angel of the Lord opened the prison gates, led the apostles out, and said to them, "Go and stand in the Temple, and tell the people all about this new life." The apostles obeyed, and at dawn they entered the Temple and started teaching.

ACTS 12:6–11 Peter is Set Free from Prison

Peter was sleeping between two guards. He was tied with two chains, and there were guards on duty at the prison gate. Suddenly an angel of the Lord stood there, and a light shone in the cell. The angel shook Peter by the shoulder, woke him up, and said, "Hurry! Get up!" At once the chains fells off Peter's hands. Then the angel said: "Fasten your belt and put on your sandals." Peter did so, and the angel said: "Put your cloak round you and come with me."

Peter followed him out of the prison, not knowing, however, if what the angel was doing was real; he thought he was seeing a vision. They passed by the first guard post and then the second, and came at last to the iron gate leading into the city. The gate opened for them by itself, and they went out. They walked down a street, and suddenly the angel left peter.

Then Peter realised what had happened to him, and said, "Now I know that it is really true! The Lord sent his angel to rescue me from Herod's power and from everything the Jewish people expected to happen."

L. 15:10 Repentance

The angels of God rejoice over one sinner who repents.

COL. 2:16–19 Fullness of Life in Christ

Let no one make rules about what you eat or drink or about holy days or the New Moon Festival or the Sabbath. All such things are only a shadow of things in the future; the reality is Christ. Do not allow yourselves to be condemned by anyone who claims to be superior because of special visions and who insists on false humility and the worship of angels. For no reason at all, such a person is puffed up by his human way of thinking and has stopped holding on to Christ, who is the head of the body. Under Christ's control the whole body is nourished and held together by its joints and ligaments, and it grows as God wants it to grow.

REV. 5:11 Millions of Angels

Again I looked, and I heard angels, thousands and millions of them!

7. HEAVEN

JOSH. 2:11 God in Heaven

The Lord your God is God in heaven above and here on earth.

1 KGS. 8:27

"But can you, O God, really live on earth? Not even all heaven is large enough to hold you."

IS. 66:1

The Lord says, "Heaven is my throne, and the earth is my footstool."

PS. 115:15–16

May you be blessed by the Lord,
who made heaven and earth!
Heaven belongs to the Lord alone,
but he gave the earth to man.

IS. 57:14–21 God's promise of Help and Healing

The Lord says, "Let my people return to me. Remove every obstacle from their path! Build the road, and make it ready!

"I am the high and holy God, who lives forever. I live in a high and holy place, but I also live with people who are humble and repentant, so that I can restore their confidence and hope. I gave my people life, and I will not continue to accuse them or be angry with them forever. I was angry with them because of their sin and greed, and so I punished them and abandoned them. But they are stubborn and kept on going their own way.

"I have seen how they acted, but I will heal them, and I will comfort those who mourn. I offer pace to all, both near and far! I will heal my people. But evil men are like the restless sea, whose waves never stop rolling in, bringing filth and muck. There is no safety for sinners," says the Lord.

MT. 3:16–17 The Baptism of Jesus

As soon as Jesus was baptized, he came up out of the water. Then heaven was opened to him, and he saw the Spirit of God coming down like a dove and alighting on him. Then a voice said from heaven, "This is my own dear Son, with whom I am pleased."

MT. 5 Teachings by Jesus

3. "Happy are those who know they are spiritually poor; the Kingdom of Heaven belongs to them!

10. "Happy are those who are persecuted because they do what God requires; the Kingdom of Heaven belongs to them!

11. "Happy are you when people insult you and persecute you and tell all kinds of evil lies against you because you are my followers. Be happy and glad, for a great reward is kept for you in heaven. This is how the prophets who lived before you were persecuted.

19–20. "Whoever disobeys event he least important of the commandments and teaches others to do the same, will be the least in the Kingdom of Heaven. On the other hand, whoever obeys the Law and teaches others to do the same, will be great in the Kingdom of Heaven. I tell you, then, that you will be able to enter the Kingdom of Heaven only if you are more faithful than the teachers of the Law and the Pharisees in doing what God requires."

14–16. "You are like a light for the whole world. A city built on a hill cannot be hidden. No one lights a lap and puts it under a bowl; instead he puts it on the lamp stand, where it gives light for everyone in the house. In the same way your light must shine before people, so that they will see the good things you do and praise your Father in heaven.

43–46. "You have heard that it was said, 'Love your friends, hate your enemies.' But now I tell you: love your enemies and pray for those who persecute you, so that you may become the sons of your Father in heaven. For he makes his sun to shine on bad and good people alike, and gives rain to those who do good and to those who do evil. Why should God reward you if you love only the people who love you? Even the tax collectors do that!"

MT. 6:19–21 Riches in Heaven

(Jesus taught) "Do not store up riches for yourselves here on earth, where moths and rust destroy, and robbers break in and steal. Instead, store up riches for yourselves in heaven, where moths and rust cannot destroy, and robbers cannot break in and steal. For your heart will always be where your riches are."

MT. 7:13–14 The Narrow Gate

"Go in through the narrow gate, because the gate to hell is wide and the road that leads to it is easy, and there are many who travel it. But the gate to life is narrow and the way that leads to it is hard, and there are few people who find it."

MT. 13:24–30 The Parable of the Weeds

Jesus told them another parable: "The Kingdom of heaven is like this. A man sowed good seed in his field. One night, when everyone was asleep, an enemy came and sowed weeds among the wheat and went away. When the plants grew and the ears of corn began to form, then the weeds showed up. The man's servants came to him and said, 'Sir, it was good seed you sowed in your field; where did the weeds come from?' 'It was some enemy who did this,' he answered. 'Do you want us to go and pull up the weeds?' they asked him. 'No,' he answered, 'because as you gather the weeds you might pull up some of the wheat along with them. Let the wheat and weeds both grow together until harvest. Then I will tell the harvest workers to pull up the weeds first, tie them in bundles and burn them, and then to gather on the wheat and put it in my barn!"

MT. 13:47–50 The Parable of the Net

"Also the Kingdom of heaven is like this. Some fishermen throw their net out in the lake and catch all kinds of fish. When the net is full, they pull it to shore and sit down to divide the fish: the good ones go into their buckets, the worthless ones are thrown away. It will be like this at the end of the age: the angels will go out and gather up the evil people from among the good and will throw them into the fiery furnace, where they will cry and grind their teeth."

MT. 18:3–4 Humility

(Jesus said) "I assure you that unless you change and become like children, you will never enter the Kingdom of heaven. The greatest in the Kingdom of heaven is the one who humbles himself and becomes like this child."

MT. 18:10–14 Parable of the Lost sheep

"See that you do not despise any of these little ones. Their angels in heaven, I tell you, are always in the presence of my Father in heaven."

"What do you think a man does who has a hundred sheep and one of them gets lost? He will leave the other ninety-nine grazing on the hillside and go and look for the lost sheep. When he finds it, I tell you, he feels far happier over this one sheep than over the ninety-nine that did not get lost. In just the same way your Father in heaven does not want any of these little ones to be lost."

MT. 19:13–14 Jesus Blesses Little Children

Some people brought children to Jesus for him to place his hands on them and to pray for them, but the disciples scolded the people. Jesus said, "Let the children come to me and do not stop them, because the kingdom of heaven belongs to such as these."

MT. 19:21–24 The Rich Young Man

Jesus said to him, "If you want to be perfect, go and sell all you have and give the money to the poor, and you will have riches in heaven; then come and follow me …"

Jesus then said to his disciples, "I assure you: it will be very hard for rich people to enter the Kingdom of heaven. I repeat: it is much harder for a rich person to enter the Kingdom of god than for a camel to go through the eye of a needle."

JN. 6:35–51 Jesus the Bread of Life

"I am the bread of life," Jesus told them. "He who comes to me will never be hungry; he who believes in me will never be thirsty. Now, I told you that you have seen me but will not believe. Everyone whom my Father gives me will come to me. I will never turn away anyone who comes to me, because I have come down from heaven to do not my own will but the will of him who sent me. And it is the will of him who sent me that I should not lose any of all those he has given me, but that I should raise them all to life on the last day …"

"I am telling you the truth: he who believes has eternal life. I am the bread of life. Your ancestors ate manna in the desert, but they died. But the bread that comes down from heaven is of such a kind that whoever eats it will not die. I am the living bread that came down from haven."

ROM. 10:11–13 Salvation is for All

The scripture says, "Whoever believes in (God) will not be disappointed." This includes everyone, because there is no difference between Jews and Gentiles; God is the same Lord of all and richly blesses all who call to him. As the scripture says, "Everyone who calls out to the Lord for help will be saved."

ROM. 10:15 Messengers of Good News

How wonderful is the coming of messengers who bring good news!

2 COR. 12:2–4 Paul's Visions

I know a certain Christian man who fourteen years ago was snatched up to the highest heaven (I do not know whether this actually happened or whether he had a vision – only God knows) ... and there he heard things which cannot be put into words, things that human lips may not speak.

EPH. 6:9 Slaves and Masters

Remember that you and your slaves belong to the same Master in heaven, who judges everyone by the same standard.

PHIL. 3:19–21 Heaven and Hell

They are going to end up in hell, because their god is their bodily desires. They are proud of what they should be ashamed of, and they think only of things that belong to this world. We, however, are citizens of heaven, and we eagerly wait for our Saviour, the Lord Jesus Christ, to come from heaven. He will change our weak mortal bodies and make them like his own glorious body, using that power by which he is able to bring all things under his rule.

1 THES. 4:16–17 The Lord's Coming

There will be the shout of command, the archangel's voice, the sound of God's trumpet, and the Lord himself will come down from heaven. Those who have died believing in Christ will rise to life first; then we who are living at that time will be gathered up along with them in the clouds to meet the Lord in the air. And so we will always be with the Lord.

2 THES. 1:6–9 Judgment at Christ's Coming

God will do what is right: he will bring suffering on those who make you suffer, and he will give relief to you who suffer and to us as well. He will do this when the Lord Jesus appears from heaven with his mighty angels, with a flaming fire, to punish those who reject God and who do not obey the Good News about our Lord Jesus. They will suffer the punishment of *eternal destruction*, separated from the presence of the Lord and from his glorious might.

PART II

DJWHAL KHUL'S TEACHINGS

(See APPENDIX for list of "Bailey Books")

Probably the most authoritative evidence available today dealing with the nature of the subjective worlds, is that which has been provided by the Master Djwhal Khul, commonly known amongst esoteric students as "D.K." or "The Tibetan".

The Tibetan's teachings have been recorded for posterity by *Alice A. Bailey*, who acted as his amanuensis. She received his instructions telepathically, and systematically committed these to writing over a period of thirty years, i.e. from 1919–1949. These communications were progressively published in 18 volumes, containing in all nearly 10,000 pages of the most advanced, inclusive and superior knowledge and wisdom concerning the life and nature of the human being, as well as the many factors affecting practically every important aspect of his subjective existence. As far as known this is the most comprehensive guide and set of instructions dealing with the nature of man's spiritual existence that has as yet been put at his disposal.

In the first chapter of this book an attempt has been made to provide a brief survey of the nature and purpose of existence, based mainly on the teachings of the Tibetan. These considerations also included some notes on the spiritual evolution of man, which should progressively prepare him to take his eventual place in the ranks of the Masters of Wisdom.

These introductory chapters (Part I) were subsequently followed by selections from some other books to provide a comparative picture of what may be expected in the hereafter. To conclude with the author again reverts to D.K.'s Teachings, with some brief notes on immortality, the nature of the etheric, astral and mental planes, as well as a few remarks on disease, death and life after death.

1

THE CONSTITUTION OF MAN

Before the question of death can be correctly understood and brought into proper perspective, it is essential that a clearer mental picture should first of all be gained about the dual nature of man.

Duality becomes apparent when spiritual forces are reduced to form or matter, giving rise to such opposites as positive and negative; life and form; light and darkness; good and evil; heaven and hell. In man these conflicting forces are expressed as Soul and personality, or the Self and the obscuring sheath of the not-Self, or the Higher Mind as opposed to the lower mind.

In the early stages of development the human consciousness remains focused in and is dominated by the physical form and its demands, and changes are only effected gradually, with the soul progressively gaining dominance over the material, emotional and selfish tendencies of the lower nature. Slowly but surely this process will continue to proceed over the ages, stretching over life after life, from youth to maturity, until the stage is eventually reached where the material existence becomes entirely absorbed or centred in the Soul, allowing the Higher Self to supersede and govern all thought and activity, thus finally leading to a state of higher unity, with the spirit supervening.

In other words, to begin with, the undeveloped individual is only aware of his physical being, which through the senses reacts to the many incentives of the environment. Such as person remains entirely orientated to the material world, satisfying the numerous bodily desires and emotions. Progressive enlightenment is only achieved as the Soul, slowly but steadily makes its presence increasingly felt, until, after a long and arduous struggle, spread over many lives, final and complete control is gained over the physical instrument. This process is paralleled with corresponding expansion in consciousness.

For present purposes the stage reached in the relationship between the Soul and its vehicle is, however, not the first consideration. What must be clearly understood is the constitution of man, and that the complete man is composed of a complicated lower body, serving as a vehicle or instrument through which the Soul effects contact with the material world. For some reason beyond human comprehension, God or Spirit must gain Physical experience, and for this purpose the Soul serves as the linking principle between Spirit and matter.

In metaphysical studies a great deal of confusion is often caused by various interpretations of the terms used. Under the circumstances it is therefore advisable to state briefly exactly what is meant when reference is here made to the "personality".

This lower vehicle is made up of three interrelated "bodies". First of all there is the dense physical body, with its vital or etheric surround; secondly there is the closely associated but intangible emotional or astral body; and thirdly, the personality is rounded off by a mental body, the impalpable surround containing the lower mind.

The Soul on the other hand is the co-ordinating principle between the spiritual and the physical. This Higher Self is the seat of the Higher Mind, and provides the channel for the divine forces of Light (Intelligence) and Love, which in the human being are translated into various aspects of consciousness.

Man's stage of development will largely be determined by the extent to which the three lower bodies, i.e. the physical, emotional and mental, have been integrated into an effective working unit known as the personality. This fusing of the lower bodies can taken place without any active participation of the Soul, and it is during this stage that the personality will show an inclination towards either the right or left hand path, depending on the extent to which the Soul has been allowed to influence the lower bodies, and to direct their activities by means of the mind.

The personality can only be regarded as fully developed, and therefore as a truly effective instrument in the hands of Higher Entities, when the Soul influences have been completely co-ordinated with the purified and integrated personality, with the Soul forces therefore pervading the lower bodies, and thus determining all activity or expressions of life, quality and form.

2

IMMORTALITY

During the past century there has been a steady accumulation of psychic and metaphysical evidence concerning the continuity of conscious existence after physical death, with a corresponding and growing awareness of the perpetual persistence of the inner human entity. The Tibetan gives us the assurance that within the next fifty years an event will take place, coupled with a revelation, which will turn the present hesitant and often sceptic attitude with regard to immortality, into one of certainty and conviction.

There are those, probably mainly influenced by Biblical interpretations, who only believe in "conditional" immortality. According to them only individuals who have accepted certain theological tenets, or have achieved a specific stage of spiritual development, will prove eligible for personal immortality, whilst those who fail in these respect are doomed either to complete annihilation, or otherwise to eternal punishment in hell. Belief in the latter state is of course also an acknowledgement of a form of immortality, but discloses either a lack of sound reflection about the meaning of eternity, or otherwise indicates a belief in a vindictive Deity, who can mete out eternal affliction for the momentary transgressions of an inadequate evolved entity briefly passing through a phase of material existence. No, this sounds absolutely illogical and will prove unacceptable to the unprejudiced thinker imbued with goodwill and a kind heart, who believes in a God of Love and who will not allow himself to be blinded by dogmatic creeds.

While pondering on these complexities of life, one is inclined to forget that each human being, qualified by his (or her) own specific characteristics, and functioning in his own particular set of circumstances, does not merely represent the coincidental product just of the present period. It expresses in fact the cumulative effect, not only of the current life episode, with its innumerable events and influences, but in addition must also be seen as the collective result of an unknown number of previous life experiences. We are therefore not only dealing with an eternal future, but at the same time with an unlimitable past. Between these two extremes the immediate life merely represents a momentary flash in the perpetual evolutionary process. Even those not prepared to accept the logic of reincarnation, must at least be aware of the effects of inherited characteristics, and of conditions and situations created by the activities experienced during previous generations.

These thoughts about immortality inevitably lead up to those ever recurring questions of *Whence, Whither, Where, When* and *Why?* Apparently such simple questions, but meanwhile impossible to answer adequately and to everybody's satisfaction, because every single individual finds himself at his own particular level of mental unfoldment, and only being able to cope with partial explanations adapted to his specific requirements. It should be remembered that there is no such thing as the Absolute Truth. All expressions of Truth are relative, and have been adapted progressively according to the gradually expanding consciousness of each individual entity.

The indiscriminate practice of spiritualism may have several drawbacks, but this movement has certainly succeeded in rendering humanity as a whole a great service by convincing a considerable part of the public of some form of survival after death. This must be considered an important step forward, but nonetheless, such survival as yet provides no final proof of immortality.

Fortunately, however, humanity is gradually becoming convinced of the fact that an indestructible element, an immortal principle, is present in each human being as a subtle and intangible entity. This is the Soul, the conveyor of consciousness, the immortal inner spiritual being, which at death withdraws from its physical vehicle, to continue its conscious existence temporarily in one of the more ethereal realms.

If it is accepted that the human spirit is immortal, and progressively evolves from stage to stage on the evolutionary ladder, systematically reaching towards every higher realms of being by unfolding its spiritual qualities, then the effect of two great natural Laws are inevitably brought to our attention. These are:

(1) The Law of Rebirth or Reincarnation, and
(2) The Law of Cause and Effect – the Law of Karma.

The Law of Rebirth maintains that the Soul, that innate spark of divinity abiding in each and every human being, is engaged on an interminable Path of Development, a Path eventually leading back to the House of the Father. This divine spark apparently needs physical experience for its proper unfoldment, and for this purpose avails itself of a human body to serve as an agent of contact with the material world. Owing to the wide range of experiences required, of which only a small part can be fitted into a single lifetime, innumerable lives or reincarnations are needed to fit in and endure all the necessary trails. From these experiences the sought-after knowledge is progressively gained, the essence of which is gleaned by the Soul, eventually to be transmuted into wisdom and perfection. After the purposes of a particular life have been accomplished and the experiences have been duly assimilated, the Soul withdraws from its temporary vehicle and establishes itself in a subjective sphere corresponding with the degree of evolvement attained. Here equally advanced entities will be encountered, and the Soul will feel at home. Apart from various service activities, it will now also have the opportunity of incorporating its recently acquired knowledge into its steadily accumulating store of wisdom.

After a shorter or longer sojourn in the world of spirit, the urge for further improvement, and therefore for fresh experiences, will again arise. With the assistance of specialised Helpers, a suitable vehicle for reincarnation will be sought, duly taking into consideration the circumstances under which the relevant infant will be born, and whether this will provide the right conditions for the satisfactory development of this particular Soul.

The basic principle underlying the Law of Karma, is that man will reap what he has sown. It is this incontrovertible truth that enables the soul to work out its own salvation in the school of life encountered during progressive incarnations, and which will step by step lead to perfection. There is nothing on earth which in the long run will prevent man from attaining his final objective – returning to the arms of the Father.

The sense of immortality, originating from the soul, comes to expression in man's instinctive tendency towards unity, an inclination which actually underlies every form of mysticism and religion. It is this same urge which drives him to seek a closer synthesis and blending with the Father – a conscious and harmonious at-one-ment with Deity. By contemplating on that which is good, true and superior, the instincts of the lower nature are overcome and translated into higher and even divine qualities and life expression.

Man's immortal existence is characterised by a constant series of deaths and subsequent resurrections, each death being the harbinger for a new life of ever increasing beauty and effectiveness. Actually each so-called death prepares the way for resurrection into some more refined sphere of activity on the ever-climbing road of attainment. At the lower levels of existence men still fear death because they unduly love and are attached to the material, where they become ensnared and entangled by their desires, their hates, and other emotional impulses or yearnings. All this is largely due to ignorance of the deeper truths and values of life, and it is only when man comes to the realisation of the true meaning of immortality with all its implications, that fear of death will gradually be dissipated.

3

THE ETHERIC WORLD

The whole Universe, with all its constituting systems and manifestations, is composed of Energy expressed

    (a)   in some tangible form or shape,
    (b)   as the intangible and invisible medium or etheric body supporting the form, and
    (c)   as the animating agent, vitalising both the form and its sustaining environment.

Creation is nothing but a vast system of mutually interdependent units of manifested energy, intimately linked together by constantly transmitted Rays of Power, originating from the SEVEN RAYS OF ENERGY. All these complexes are constantly vivified, conditioned or modified by receiving energy from outer sources, and thus in turn being enabled to give out or radiate forces for supporting certain aspects of that which is less evolved. This is a never-ending performance which by means of the all-permeating Etheric Web is proceeding perpetually on every plane of activity.

In this connection it should also be remembered that man, even with the assistance of the wonderful scientific equipment of today, can nevertheless as yet only become aware of a negligible part of the physically manifested macrocosm. Beyond this, but still closely associated with the physical worlds, apparently lies, as far as man is concerned, not only the largely unexplored and unknown vast etheric worlds, but also successive realms of spirit of ever increasing refinement and beatitude. Yes, man still has a long way to go!

Each body of manifestation, whether an atom or a solar system is contained within its etheric counterpart. The etheric body consists of a network of minute or major interlacing channels of energy, serving the dual purpose of reception of outer energies, and the radiation and distribution of forces generated from within the body. This vital body therefore actually controls and conditions the related physical form.

As a practical demonstration, let us start with the atom. The atom represents an organised unit in which certain mutually attracted energies have been concentrated and are enclosed by an atom wall. This wall is supported by an "electric" surround, known as the etheric body. The energies contained within the atom remain in constant circulation. As no atom wall is, however, absolutely impervious to energy, there is always some degree of percolation and an interchange of energy in both directions – i.e. both inwards and outwards.

Each atom should be regarded as a minute but living entity. It breathes in by absorbing energy from the outer etheric network, and which has been derived from surrounding sources. The assimilated energy serves to vivify and condition the energies already contained within the atom. But the atom also breathes out by radiating forces from its own store of energy into the encircling etheric body for transmission into the wider etheric surround, thus contributing its small share of influence towards affecting its environment.

As is well known in nature, atoms are grouped together into an infinite variety of larger units, providing in the diverse needs of manifestation. With the building of larger units, the etheric surround of individual atoms is retained, thus fulfilling the dual function of acting as a binding medium between the atoms, and simultaneously serving as channels of communication and distribution of energy. Each manifested material body, and therefore also the body of man, is thus interpenetrated right down to atomic levels with an etheric network, securely contained in an outer etheric surround which follows the contours of the body concerned and therefore closely resembles the enclosed physical form.

ONE WHOLE

All intermediate etheric bodies are again linked with neighbouring etheric complexes, and this process is extended until eventually the etheric surround of every form of creation, from the most minute to the very largest, is included into a vast single unit. This framework does not only apply to our Earth, but also stretches out to include every other planet, our solar system, every other heavenly body, system or galaxy, and finally embracing all of Creation, linking the entire Universe into one vast interdependent WHOLE.

The result of this huge inter-communicating scheme is that each and every form of creation is directly or indirectly connected with every other manifestation by this unending etheric network. Therefore, theoretically speaking, the vibration caused by an action in any one part must inevitably be passed on to have some effect on every other part. It stands to reason, however, that minor vibrations will with increasing distance be inclined to fade out, eventually becoming quite unnoticeable. On the other hand the Earth, with all it contains, is definitely affected by rays and vibrations, not only from our Sun and the rest of our planetary system, but also by radiations reaching us from the outer Cosmos.

MAN'S ETHERIC BODY

But let us revert to the etheric aspects of the human body.

The etheric system is the medium through which the life forces are directed, serving not only as the receiver of these forces, but also as assimilator and transmitter. The consequence is that if for some reason or other the etheric body is withdrawn from its physical counterpart, then life in this body at the same time also becomes extinguished, and death sets in with its associated processes of disintegration.

In the case of a human being the final link of the etheric body with the physical, is an interlaced cord of etheric matter terminating in the spleen, and known as the "Silver Cord". When this cord is disrupted the connection with the dense physical body is broken, and the etheric body set free, for the time being only remaining linked with its corresponding astral body. But more about this at a later stage.

As already pointed out the etheric body consists of a network of energy threads and membranes interpenetrating the whole physical organism down to atomic levels. This network, however, also extends beyond the periphery of the form to produce an enfolding surround of energy. This etheric cloak or "Aura" will vary considerably from person to person, not only in thickness and brightness, but also in colour, thus providing by the nature of its radiation or appearance a direct reflection of the consciousness and evolutionary state attained by the conditioning entity. The inner network is again closely associated with the nervous system, which it feeds, controls and galvanises into action.

The aura or "sphere of radiation" is characterised by seven focal points of energy, known as the seven "Energy Centres", which in turn are closely related to the principal internal organs. Of these seven centres, two are located in the head and give along the spine. The seven vital centres are linked with each other by lines of force, and these also serve to establish contact with the nervous system, as well as with the environing etheric system. The effective response of the etheric vehicle, and therefore also the physical condition and health of a person, are directly dependent on the condition of the centres and their capacity to appropriate, utilise and transmit available energies.

The whole Universe, and more particularly as far as man is concerned, our whole Earth is vitalised and pervaded by One Life, revealing itself as energy pouring through and stimulating to activity every single form of manifestation in every kingdom of nature. The only fundamental difference between the many forms of creation, is that of consciousness, and in this respect it is only the human being and higher Entities who dispose of *self*-consciousness, which is the product of the incarnating Soul.

Each manifested body, whether recognised as a separate unit or otherwise as a form within a form, must be regarded as a living entity. Whether realised or not, every so-called unit constitutes part of a greater unit. All these units are more or less intimately linked and related by their individual etheric surrounds, thus vibrating and reacting to mutually emanating impulses, yet each being characterised by its own qualifying life, by its own particular colouring and its own specific type of consciousness. It is the nature of this indwelling consciousness which will finally determine the quality of the form, rendering it either magnetic or repudiating, receptive or transmitting.

All forms are therefore imbued and animated by the One Life, but are limited in time and space by the nature, quality and evolutionary state of the indwelling Consciousness.

To avoid confusion it might just be mentioned that in esoteric literature a distinction is sometimes made between the meaning of the terms "force" and "energy". As a rule emanations from matter or form are referred to as "force", whilst those originating from the more subjective spheres are known as "energy". This distinction is of course only relative.

EVOLUTION AND DESTRUCTION OF FORM

The secret of evolution lies in the destruction of the material aspect. Life remains imprisoned in the physical vehicle only until the objective of Higher Entities has been achieved. When this stage has been reached, the life energy is withdrawn by means of the etheric system and destruction of the form proceeds, allowing the constituting parts, i.e. atoms and stored energy, to be absorbed by either the material or etheric surround. In nature this process is never ending. At times it proceeds rapidly and spectacularly, but as a rule the activity is gradual and inconspicuous, but nonetheless effective. New forms are constantly being constructed, and will be provided as and when required by the divine Plan, to be maintained subsequently for as long as needed for achieving the objectives of the Plan. When their purpose has been served, or when the form begins to exert a restricting influence on expansion and development, destruction will again be effected. After rejection of that which has become redundant, the released energy will seek new forms of expression. The rapidity of these changes will keep pace with the evolutionary urge and the state of the awakening consciousness. But change there always will be and must be, because energy can never become immobilised. Every form of manifestation, whether apparent to human observation or not, remains in a perpetual state of change, this being one of the inexorable Laws of Nature.

The dense physical human body as such is the relatively inanimate instrument automatically responding to the impulses received through its inclusive vital body. This body represents the aggregate product of the energies from various sources, which at any one time are focused through the seven etheric centres. It is the condition of these centres which will provide a true reflection of the evolutionary attainment of the individual concerned.

The development attained might tentatively be grouped into fours stages, all finding expression through the etheric body:

1. That of the unevolved savage, still mainly responsive to life forces of a material nature, stimulating the physical appetites and instincts. The intellect at this stage remains fairly dormant, and activities are primarily prompted by the five senses.
2. That of the average human being still under active domination of his astral body, and therefore remaining in the first instance motivated by emotion and desire. These astral forces animating the etheric body, lead to conflicts between confronting pairs of opposites. Because the vast majority of humanity is at present still under domination of astral influences, the vital body is mainly being used for the expression of astral energy.
3. Once the three lower bodies have become integrated in the personality, the mental body gradually gains control over the astral influences, thus allowing the etheric body to become increasingly governed by thought energy. In the early stages activities will, however, still tend towards selfish desire, but this inclination will steadily be superseded by mental considerations.
4. The stage when the Soul gains dominance over the integrated personality, allowing the inspired mind to take command. This results in the Soul-infused personality, serving the Divine Plan under guidance of the Hierarchy. This means that the aspirant is treading the Path of Light by the effective control of his etheric vehicle.

As soon as the inner man's attention becomes focused on higher values, the forces brought into play through the etheric body engender conflict between the physical inclinations of the lower bodies and the more refined trends of the higher nature. It is during this stage that the accent begins to be placed on such disciplines as physical hygiene and exercise, on celibacy, abstinence, vegetarianism and general moderation concerning various demands of the physical instrument. In other words the aspirant accepts the challenge and becomes engaged in the battle between the pairs of opposites.

Many of the causes of physical disease or of psychological disturbances can be traced directly to either over-stimulation of the vital body, or to under-development of certain of the seven energy-centres of the etheric body. These are in turn closely associated and are directly responsible for the effective functioning of the endocrine system.

The following may be regarded as the principal relationships of the vital body:

1. The vital body is basically the receiver and the transmitter of both universal and localised energies.
2. The etheric body not only surrounds the form, but also interpenetrates it, thus underlying the physical structure and forming the counterpart of both the nervous and glandular systems.
3. The glands of the endocrine system are the material reflections of both the major and minor energy-centres.
4. As the terminal part of the nervous system, the brain represents the centre of consciousness, whilst the heart may be regarded as the centre of life aspect, by circulating the vital forces through the blood stream.

The sound functioning of the physical vehicle is mainly dependent on four controlling systems:

1. The *vital or etheric system*, working through seven major energy centres, twenty-one lesser centres, and forty-nine smaller centres.
2. The *endocrine system*, closely associated with the etheric system, and also represented by seven major glands, and many of lesser

importance which may be regarded as the counterpart to the corresponding etheric centres.

3. The *nervous system*, also supported by the etheric system, terminating in the brain, and intimately affiliated with the blood stream.

4. The *blood stream* is the carrier of the life principle, and to a large extent is the distributor of energies, forces or secretions derived from the previous three systems.

Apart from the steams of energy originating from outer spheres of influence, there are five principal sources of localised energy constantly pouring into the human vital body and conditioning the physical vehicle. Of these the two major energies emanate from the Soul and from the Personality. These two energies are then qualified by three subsidiary streams of force derived from the mental nature, the astral body, and the dense physical body. A growing interest is at present becoming noticeable in the medical profession with regard to the importance of the etheric body, and the significant role it is playing in the health of man. The time is rapidly approaching when these effects will be fully realised, and when the attention of medical men will become primarily focused on a study and consideration of the etheric vehicle for combating disease and for the general improvement of health conditions.

4

THE ASTRAL WORLD

Those who believe in the existence of an astral world, are as yet seldom aware of the fact that this intangible world is actually unreal, purely a figment of the imagination, and therefore a sphere of illusion. Nonetheless, although it may sound paradoxical, for the person who has self-created this world of delusion, it remains very real indeed. Similarly it must also have played an important role during the aeons of his previous existence. It will furthermore continue to exert a dominant influence on his future activities until, by means of his mental efforts, he finally succeeds in raising himself out of these murky spheres of glamour and distortion into the clearer light of the mental plane. Only when this stage has been achieved, will the aspirant be able to realise that for many lives he has been struggling with curtailed vision in the mists and obscurity of the emotional world. Only then will he progressively begin to truly recognise the astral plane for what it essentially represents – an imaginary sphere of deception, of self-created chimeras and illusions, from which the average man finds it extremely difficult to escape. Such release can only be affected after persistent effort during the course of many lives, and stimulated by the steadfast support of the light of the Soul directed through the mind.

In due course each human being, with the active assistance of his Soul, has to arrive within himself to a clearer conception of the nature of the astral or emotional plane. Through his self-initiated struggles, he will over the course of several lives, gradually have to release himself from its tenacious hold, by systematically following a path of distancing himself from all association with the urges and desires of the phenomenal life. Astral awareness represents a state of consciousness which must progressively be radically modified.

To effect this inner transformation, man must realise that the astral plane is not something that is divinely inspired, but is merely the illusory product of human desire, fabricated and accumulated since the dawn of man's intelligence. From these cravings have resulted thought-forms corresponding with every phase of desire, ranging from the lowest physical impulses up to the spiritual aspirations of those who have become aware of the first glimmerings of Light, and have taken the first hesitant steps on the path towards perfection. Simultaneously a growing urge will be developed to overcome the innate selfishness of the less evolved nature, and to become of some practical service to fellow men. This tendency originates from the heart and mind, is inspired by the Soul, and is implemented by the will.

What is known as the astral plane is nothing but the sum-total of the sensory and emotional reactions, with their attending thought-forms, which have been accumulated over the ages. These are man's own creations which have been effectively projected on to his etheric surround. Since immemorial times he has been the victim of this false, distorted and deceptive subjective world of his own construction. This world of glamour has been tolerated by Divine Power because it provides evolving man with the right circumstances and an effective terrain for gaining the necessary experience which eventually will enable him to distinguish between the false and the true, finally leading him to the reality of the realms of Spirit.

Within each and every human being there dwells a latent Power, variously known as the "Love of God", as the "Christ Within", or simply as the Soul, which has always been present, but has not asserted itself during the early stages of the evolutionary process, except by providing man with some degree of self-consciousness. Only after numerous lives have been expended in gaining experience while living in intimate contact with the dense physical world with its many fields of desire and emotional expression, is the phase reached when the Soul slowly begins to respond, gradually making its presence felt. Eventually the time will arrive when during certain lives it will start dominating the lower vehicles of expression and thus asserting the "Quality of Life". This latter stage indicates that the pilgrim is finding his way back to the House of the Father.

This process whereby the striver is gradually freeing himself from the shackles which during the past held the Soul subordinated to the dictates of the lower vehicles and the suffocating and depressing influence of the astral plane, is not only of benefit to himself, but at the same time will prove to be of considerable service to his fellow men. His self-centred forces, his personal desires and sensual inclinations of the past, will become transmuted into more refined energies, leading to expressions of tolerance, goodwill and loving understanding of his associates.

The primary characteristic of the astral plane is its glamour. It is on this plane that the confrontation between the pairs of opposites takes place, and where the ensuring battles between such attributes as good and evil, love and hate, selfish desire and altruistic sharing, are concluded. The stage will eventually be reached when the strength of the Soul will overcome the glamour and negative inclinations of the lower nature, with a growing aspiration to freedom of expression and liberation from every form of astral control.

For the members of the Spiritual Hierarchy, the Masters, the astral plane no longer exists. As pointed out this plane is in reality fictitious and merely the illusory product of the lower mind of man. As the individual during the course of his spiritual unfoldment, releases himself from these illusions by raising his consciousness, these astral miasmas are gradually dispersed as far as he himself is concerned. For those still lagging behind, the reality of these obscuring forces however remains unaltered, until they in their turn finally succeed in surmounting these obstructions, realising that the astral plane has no true existence and merely represents a self-erected structure.

Normally man, while still functioning in his physical body, remains consciously unaware of the astral world by which he is surrounded. Actually physical man is separated from this intangible astral world by what is known as the "etheric web" which as a rule cannot be readily penetrated by those still gaining their experience in dense matter.

There are many psychic mediums who are working under the

delusive impression that they are in contact with the spiritual realms, and are receiving messages or instruction from the higher spheres where the Spiritual Hierarchy is to be found. In the majority of instances, especially in the case of trance mediums, their clairvoyance or clair-audience, however, does not stretch beyond the astral plane, and the reported phenomena are therefore of a purely astral nature. These mystics may be entirely honest and truthful in what they report, but because they have not yet reached the stage where they can accurately relate and interpret that which they are registering, and are as yet unqualified to distinguish the spurious from the genuine, or illusion from the real, they and their customers are often severely deluded. The results of these astral contacts may at times prove beautiful and even inspiring, but nevertheless they must still be regarded with distrust and can usually be recognised by their highly emotional nature.

The trouble is how to distinguish truly between the spurious and the authentic, the deceptive and the genuine? This will always remain a problem, but in this respect a few simple rules may be followed, which may not provide an absolute safeguard, but will nevertheless prove of considerable help.

In the first instance carefully guard against any form of spiritual arrogance, and try to foster a spirit of inner humility in every form of mystical approach. There is so often the tendency to regard oneself as a special or chosen delegate, or as a mouthpiece of the Masters. This may readily lead to unnecessary cleavages, to pride and presumption, and to a lack of recognition of the many facets of expression of the One Work.

Secondly, messages which directly concern the personality or are in any way inclined to raise the recipient to some pedestal, should always be regarded with suspicion. The work of the Hierarchy is comprehensive, and the true server should realise that there are numerous workers distributed over a wide field, and that activities are taking place on many levels and many spheres of expression. Each worker is accorded his own specific function, which will correspond with his capacities as determined by his particular stage of development and his individual characteristics and qualifications. But notwithstanding the great variety of activities, all these servers form part of the One Hierarchy, are held together by the bonds of Divine Love and Light, and collectively strive towards the realisation of the One Objective.

Thirdly, workers should see to it that they are as far as possible released from every form of physical desire and emotional instigations. This may be achieved by subjecting all activities to mental and eventually to soul-control. In dealing with the general public it may at times prove advisable to avail oneself of restrained emotional approaches, but the server should ensure that he personally remains free from these emotional associations.

Whatever one's approach or objectives in life, it should always be kept in mind that the vast majority of human being are still predisposed to and activated by influences and forces arising from the astral plane. These astral forces however vary widely in quality and potency, and may represent impulses of either a sordid or a refined nature, and depending on the magnetic qualities of the individual, they will differ considerably in effect. These differences will further become accentuated by the extent to which mental control is being brought into play to subdue, moderate or direct the relative forces.

The astral plane has always been known as the "watery realm", with water as its symbol. Its typical characteristics are its instability, its fluid and stormy nature, and it evidences the same distortionary effects as when looking through a watery medium.

Finally there is the obscuring quality of its mists and fogs. But just as water remains an essential ingredient for human existence, so its astral counterpart forms a closely associated feature of the outgoing Piscean Age, and will similarly be intimately related to the incoming Aquarian Age, with the "water-carrier" as its symbol.

The emotional plane also forms the temporary habitat of discarnate lives, where they transiently abide, either while passing out of incarnation, or otherwise on their way towards incarnation. These aspects will, however, be discussed in greater detail at a later stage.

THE ASTRAL BODY

Just as the human etheric body forms a minute part of the vast etheric structure, so individual astral bodies of human beings are component parts of the astral plane. Where the human physical body is permeated with and enshrouded by its etheric or vital body, so this complex is in turn enclosed in an astral or emotional surround of less clearly defined outline.

No esoteric student can make satisfactory progress until a reasonable concept can be formed of the nature of the astral plane and of his own astral vehicle. Without soul contact there can, however, be no clear understanding of these problems. He then has to learn how to free himself from these emotional agencies, and at the same time how to make effective use of these powers. For this purpose he has to acquire the necessary discrimination by efficiently applying his mental powers. He must come to the realisation that the astral plane is the realm where the emotions have free play and dominate all expression; that it is the plane of illusion, glamour and distortion, but that it nevertheless is the sphere in which the average human being unconsciously moves and exists, constantly struggling to disentangle himself from the surrounding confusion of interacting emotional forces. His problem is to find the right clue by means of which he will systematically be able to free and then to raise himself from this maze. For this purpose he must learn to distinguish the truth from that which is false, and the permanent from the transient.

Every individual who finally succeeds in liberating himself from the stifling effects of this world of illusion, not only has reached an important milestone on his personal road of development, but by such progress he is also contributing his share towards freeing enslaved mankind as a whole.

In man the battle between the opposites, between light and darkness, good and evil, is fought out in the emotional body. The more advanced the worker, the more sensitive his astral body will become to outer influences. This therefore represents a truly reciprocal reaction, because while the physical body is becoming increasingly refined and sentient, this will be reflected in an emotional body of constantly growing potency.

The most demanding task of the aspirant lies in the effective curbing of his emotional nature, and this can only be achieved with the help of the Soul. This is the stage where he becomes aware of that inner sense of duality, of the contending forces within him, which are pulling him hither and thither between opposing poles of tension. After having remained relatively dormant for aeons and through the activities of numerous incarnations, the Soul now has definitely awakened and is asserting itself by beginning to play a more active role. Through the light of his Soul the aspirant is becoming aware of the murky darkness of his astral surround, and the struggle is engaged between good and evil, between the forces of light emanating from the Soul and the forces of darkness, of lust and selfish desire arising from the lower vehicles of expression. The deciding factor in this grim struggle, often stretching over several lives, is the Divine Will, asserting itself through the Soul, and contending against the selfish will of the personality. This struggle may prove long and arduous, but the fight is nevertheless unequal and heavily weighted in favour of the forces contending for the good, which in the end are inevitably bound to gain the upper hand.

In this battle the individual as such is actively concerned and cannot play the role of an interested but idle bystander. It is for him to choose whether his unfoldment is going to be slow or whether he is going to throw in his weight with the higher forces, or whether he is going to temporise by at first acceding to the attractive forces and temptations of the lower nature. The latter procedure would only mean the prolonging of his painful struggle, until eventually he becomes aware of the light and attractions of the higher realms and decides to follow the "Path of Return" by reacting positively to the dictates of his Soul.

After honest self-evaluation the student should decide for himself what approximate stage of progress he had attained. It may be considered that the average man is still mainly engaged in the control and disciplining of his physical body. The next step is when the worker finds himself on the probationary path. He now becomes aware of his astral body and must learn to subdue and suitably direct the forces of his emotional nature. This is followed by the stage when the astral body, with its variety of sensual and desire impulses, has been brought under reasonable mental control, and through the mind is reacting to the directions of the Soul. The path of accepted discipleship has now been entered and the worker is beginning to serve as a useful instrument on behalf of the elder Brothers.

CONTROLLING FORCES

Generally speaking the variety of forces animating the astral body may be classified into three main groups.

Firstly, there are the many forms of expression of selfish desire which in the early stages of man's development are largely responsible for his activities. The urges generated by desire are, as a rule, extremely difficult to overcome, and this process will consequently only proceed slowly and will usually be spread progressively over several lifetimes.

The second comprehensive group of forces generally affecting those still dominated by the astral worlds, is that which is included under the several aspects of fear; that cruel element, with which every normal person is so well acquainted in the course of daily life, ever devising new ways of manifesting itself, and so often the cause of undue pain and unhappiness. As a generalisation it may be said that fear is frequently engendered and nourished by ignorance. It is basically instinctual, as evidenced in the animal world, where fear fulfils an important function in self-preservation. In the case of human beings, fear, instead of being moderated, actually becomes aggravated by being subjected to man's mental powers. His imagination is brought into play, allowing him to visualise every unpleasant possibility. To this must furthermore be added the memory aspect by recalling painful experiences of the past; by means of his powers of association and anticipation the forces relating to his fears are exaggerated, thereby accentuating and magnifying their potency beyond all reason. This is because "energy follows thought", and therefore by paying undue attention to his anxieties, man's whole life may become dominated by quite unjustified thought-forms of what might lie in store for him.

To the uninformed, one of his worst fears remains that of death. Again this must largely be ascribed to ignorance and a fear of the unknown. He does not know what lies in store for him and is secretly frightened by the visualised perpetual burning in the fires of hell with which he has been threatened since early youth. Although he might profess not to believe in these stories about hell, there nevertheless often remains a shadow of uncertainty, even if unacknowledged, which is inclined to generate a fear complex.

The third group of forces commonly encountered on the astral plane is that caused by sex attraction, originating from physical desire. Basically it may be described as the attractive force evidenced between spirit and matter, manifesting itself as the urge to unite male and female in order to procreate. This instinct towards propagation forms part of the evolutionary pattern of nature, and it is only when this natural tendency becomes perverted by emotional desire in the case of man, that it can no longer be justified and must be regarded as a sign of degeneration.

These three groups of astral forces, namely that of selfish desire, the many forms of fear, and uncontrolled sexual urges, can all be brought under mental control when effectively guided by the Soul.

DEPRESSION

A further typical and all to common evidence of astral domination occurs when the personality is allowed to fall into a state of depression. This is a plight to which every normal individual remains subject to a lesser or greater degree during the course of his chequered life. During such a phase, which may vary considerably in intensity, man surrounds himself with a miasma of emotionalism, thereby blurring his reasoning faculties, and making it impossible to distinguish clearly or to take the needed steps with confidence and discrimination.

The cause of this illusionary state may be either due to ruling world conditions, or to the circumstances to which the individual happens to be exposed. These conditions may in turn arise either from physical situations or psychological factors.

As long as man allows his life to be identified with his astral body, permitting himself to be controlled by his moods and feelings, or by yielding to his lusts and desires, he will also remain subject to periods of doubt and despair, to deep depression and misery. To counter these deprimating influences, his approach to life should be founded on the three broad principles of *right speech, thought* and *purpose*. With the proper and successful attention to these tenets, the aspirant will find that his whole outlook and attitude of mind will become radically changed. These principles will find expression in daily life in the many forms of goodwill towards fellow men, as loving understanding of the problems of others, and right activity in serving one's neighbours and humanity as a whole, and last but not the least, in helping our Elder Brothers with the realising of their objectives.

EBB AND FLOW OF ENERGY

All forms of energy and force are subject to more or less regular cyclic manifestations. This ebb and flow can be observed in all life processes, and is especially noticeable in man, resulting in alternating periods of light and darkness, of joy and misery, of exaltation and depression. Once the aspirant becomes consciously aware of this process and begins to subject these forces to mental control, a more even trend can, however, be achieved, with the high and low levels less accentuated. Man, with his free will, can therefore establish himself at a midway point of these cyclic occurrences, thus enabling him at least partly to subdue the forces responsible for the fluctuating movements.

It should be realised, however, that these vacillating states are due to the fact that the consciousness is still largely focused in the physical and astral bodies instead of in the Soul. Once the consciousness can be raised and steadily centred in the Soul, the soul-infused man will be affected to a minimum by alternating surrounding forces and conditions, thus enabling him to achieve a firm stand in "spiritual being".

Like every other sphere of existence the astral realm also consists of undefined and merging lower and higher regions. The lower spheres are characterised by darkness and denseness of atmosphere, which will progressively become lighter and more tenuous as the higher astral regions are attained. But as already pointed out, the astral world is self-created and the conditions encountered after taking leave of the physical vehicle, will solely depend on the nature of the life that has been led, whether purely selfish or tending towards goodwill and altruism, and the resulting state of consciousness. Furthermore, the phase of development attained by the relative entity will also determine the length of his sojourn in the astral regions, whether he is going to remain there until his next incarnation or whether his stay is only of a temporary nature while on his way to higher realms.

5

THE MENTAL PLANE

In metaphysical studies reference is constantly made to various subjective bodies associated with the physical vehicle, and which collectively constitute the "personality". Actually it is only in the case of the vital body, which in contour intimately conforms to its dense physical counterpart, that we are really justified in alluding to this intangible energy surround as a "body". In the case of the astral body we are dealing with a body of illusion, which under certain circumstances may, however, assume proportions closely resembling the physical form, but which nevertheless remains delusive and a product of the imagination or thought life. The mental body is something even more vague and intangible, and must rather be regarded as a focal sphere of influence closely affiliated with and forming an integral part of the personality. It is the field where the relative mental energies are brought into contact, and interacting produce impulses which serve to activate and control the associated physical body.

Through study, concentration and meditation the student proceeds on to mental levels. With increasing success he learns to create thought-forms, to pervade these forms with energy and to send them forth, directly them to fulfil some specific purpose. The adequacy and potency of the form concerned will depend on the student's clarity of vision and the depth of his inner realisation. In the early stages of mental development, where the majority of men still find themselves, the thought processes are still relatively undefined, resulting in obscure and confused thought-forms which are feeble and ineffective, and are therefore unable to produce clear-cut results. These workers should instead aim at improving their powers of rapid thought concentration, the construction of more distinct thought-forms, giving greater care to the final manifesting of these visions, thus resulting in greater creative proficiency. Once the attention of the thinker is adequately focused on the mental plane, the results of his application will become certain and inevitable.

What a pity that so few are as yet consciously aware of the potency of the mental forces which are at their disposal and which can be so effectively applied for the benefit of man. Apparently man is, however, destined to become increasingly aware of his intellectual heritage, and in the years to come more and more workers will avail themselves of these mental capacities, to the growing advantage of mankind as a whole.

THE MENTAL BODY

Each personality is supported by a mental body. During the early phases of man's development his body remains rudimentary, hardly playing any role at all. At this stage activities will largely be determined by instinctive and emotional impulses. It is only with the gradual unfoldment of the lower concrete mind that the mental body will progressively begin to assume more definite proportions, and to fulfil a more active function in daily life. In due course however, the time will arrive when decisions will no longer be determined by emotional factors, but solely by mental considerations.

The refinement of the mental body will essentially depend on concentrated and persistent effort combined with sound discrimination. It will require unobscured thinking and the capacity of formulating, directing and clearly defining thought-matter. In other words the capacity must be cultivated of constructing well-defined thought-forms, and of effectively directing and applying such forms to achieve the required objective. For this purpose it is first of all essential that the mental body should be made suitably receptive to the energy impulses from the Soul by stilling all turbulent inclinations which periodically might still tend to emanate from the astral body. This may be achieved by sustained efforts at concentration and meditation, practised over the course of many years.

It should be pointed out that during this process of self-induced mental refinement, no undue attention should be paid to constant self-analysis, nor should there be strained efforts to attain results. Such progress can never be rapid and neither can it be hurried. It will therefore inevitably take time, so it is advisable to forget about the personal aspects as far as possible, by concentrating the attention on service activities on behalf of fellow men. Such work, if systematically and unselfishly maintained, will unfailingly ensure steadfast mental growth and unfoldment.

As far as these efforts are concerned, one of the most difficult problems to cope with is to bring the emotional body under proper restraint, and to bring the refractory elements of the lower nature under reasonable mental control, and thus to encourage an inner state of serenity and stability, with the conviction that complete reliance may be placed on the guidance of the Soul and of that of Higher Entities.

In preparing the mental body for effective service, it should be supplied systematically with the knowledge and facts required for its intellectual and scientific unfoldment. Such information will also serve to provide a sound foundation for the eventual transmutation of such knowledge into Divine Wisdom.

THE MIND

The question may be asked how to distinguish between the astral plane and the mental plane – between emotion and thought.

Sound discrimination, which is a quality of the mind, is as yet largely lacking in the case of the majority of humanity. It is by means of this attribute that the difference between emotion and thought can best be distinguished. Emotion results from sensory perception, from feeling. On the other hand, feeling can produce no emotion without the presence of a certain degree of mental awareness; that is, thought currents must give direction or meaning to feeling. It is therefore the interaction of feeling and thought that is known as emotion. If feeling remains undirected it gives rise to various forms of glamour and illusion, and these fogs can only be dispelled when subjected to the discriminating and clarifying attributes of the discerning mind.

One of the basic attributes of the mind is its aptitude of visualising, of building images or thought-forms from emotional experiences. A clear line of demarcation between mind, thought and emotion of feeling can, however, not be drawn. They are all manifestations of life, are interacting, but nonetheless occur at different levels. Thus the higher mind emanates from the Soul, and it is by means of its intelligent powers of thought that the observer learns to distinguish between the inner subjective qualities of his immortal Soul and the sensory and emotional qualities of the physical vehicle. Because of the subjective nature of these higher principles, words adapted to descriptions of the physical world can never provide a satisfactory explanation of these differences, and it is only through the intuitional faculties of the higher mind that the student will arrive at reasonably satisfactory inner conclusions.

The mental body serves as the abode of the mind, the intellect or consciousness. As far as this concept is concerned it should be clearly realised that the brain is not the actual seat of the mind, but merely represents its physical instrument in the form of a wonderful computer, of which the mind avails itself.

A clear distinction should be made between the nature and functions of the Lower or Concrete Mind and its complement the Higher or Abstract Mind. The concrete mind is a direct product of the physical brain and is therefore of transitory nature, whereas the abstract mind is associated with the Soul, representing a permanent and indestructible principle, which persistently gains a stronger influence during the evolutionary process of the personality, through which it happens to express itself.

Mind is that faculty of consciousness which lends itself to logical deduction and reasoning, which eventually should lead to rational activity. It is this talent which distinguishes the human from the animal kingdom. The mind also provides the key by means of which man may gain entrance to the fifth kingdom of nature – the spiritual world. This will eventually be effected by converting the discriminative faculty of the mind to the intuitive.

Mind may also be regarded as the discriminating will and the directing purpose which will finally determine the life-course of every self-conscious and intelligent human being. It is the principle by means of which the active Will of some Higher Entity finds expression through its constituting elements – the puny lives of men. These are concepts which in many respects range beyond the understanding of the normal intellect, and it is only as the lower mind is gradually transmuted to the higher, and then eventually to the intuition, that its real significance will become more apparent. This will entail a graded expansion of consciousness on the upward path of mental and spiritual evolution, successively passing through ever more exalted planes of existence.

The objective which unconsciously faces evolving man, is the bridging of the gap between the concrete and abstract minds, eventually leading to their mutual interaction and a benign synthesis with the higher mind in command.

One of the outstanding characteristics of the lower mind is its power of discrimination. It is through this attribute that the domination of the emotional life, with its many disturbing qualities, is steadily overcome. Such mastery results in some degree of stability and restfulness, which will permit the percolation of a certain amount of Light from higher levels, allowing the real to be distinguished from illusion, and the Self from the not-Self. The higher abstract mind is therefore the carrier of Light and the instrument of illumination, providing those still struggling in the world of matter with the "lighted way" to higher objectives.

While the lower mind is still in command, it tends to contribute to an inordinate feeling of self-sufficiency, to mental arrogance, and consequently to separativeness. This can only be countered effectively by the magnetic qualities of *Love*. Therefore that which the mind is inclined to separate, must be linked and merged again by the energies of Love. No barriers can in the long run withstand the constant onslaughts of Love, so with this power at one's disposal, that which has been disrupted by astral forces can be restored, soothed and healed again by the all-embracing energy of Love. True and intelligent Love can only be recognised and attained after the mind has first of all been effectively developed and man becomes consciously aware of himself as the Soul, only temporarily availing itself of a physical instrument.

Humanity has entered a mental era where intelligent use of the concrete mind is steadily gaining ground and is overcoming the astral forces of desire and uncontrolled emotional expression which characterised such a large part of human's activity in the past. From now on man's attitudes and performances will increasingly be determined by his powers of thought, and will to a far lesser extent be guided by purely physical and emotional considerations. How important therefore that there should be a clearer understanding of the forces involved and that the mind should become attuned to the Soul, whose nature is consistently qualified by intelligent Love.

Man's mental development is normally characterised by three states:

(a) the early phase during which the mind still mainly receives its impressions from the surrounding physical or astral worlds through the five senses which register their impulses in the brain. The resulting reactions will consequently be primarily emotional and concerned with the needs, desires and urges of the lower bodies.

(b) The second stage is that during which the mind, through its own intelligent reasoning capacity, arrives at its own conclusions. The intellect, with its thought life, therefore becomes the controlling factor, with the emotional considerations receding into the background. The reasoning principle is brought into play when knowledge, acquired by physical and emotional experience, is mentally co-ordinated.

(c) The decisive stage is reached when the Soul, after playing a secondary role for aeons, finally succeeds through concentration and meditation, in imposing its objectives upon the mind, which has become receptive and responsive to its impressions originating from spiritual realms.

The final struggle for mastery by the Soul will be fought out in the astral body, and for this purpose the decisive weapon will prove to be the dedicated mind. The mental plane is also the field where the soul succeeds in making direct contact with the form aspect. What the worker should strive for in order to realise some specific objective, is to gain that degree of conscious control that will enable him to focus his consciousness at will either in his Soul or in his form aspect.

To make the proper use of his mental faculties, man must first of all learn to think correctly, and how to make the most effective use of his thought-apparatus. It is by means of sustained right thinking of the masses and by knowing how to utilise mental energy correctly, that progressive evolution of the human race will continue.

Sound thinking will be subject to several factors. To begin with the talent of suitable appraisal of "the vision" must be acquired, which will entail a measure of conscious awareness and sensitivity to impressions from the subjective spheres. At a later stage this will be evidenced by a periodic flashing forth of the intuition. With the developing of this aptitude, sources of power will be tapped which belong to the succeeding plane of intuition. Once the observer has sensed an inkling of the beauty of the Divine Plan, he will be granted the opportunity of bringing as much of this Plan as he can cope with down to the mental level where he is currently functioning. As far as lies within his power, he can then proceed to convert these supernal ideas into suitable thought-forms. How fortunate those who finally succeed in materialising something of this vision on the earth plane, thus enabling humanity as a whole to share in this bequest from On High.

The mind should be regarded as a focal point of pure Light, as a powerful reflector of the Light of the Soul, thereby endowing man with some discernment of supernal Wisdom. The mind, the vehicle of thought, should therefore become the instrument of the Soul, for conveying as much of the Light and Love of the Soul as the mental body can handle. It is by means of the illumined mind that the mists of illusion are dispelled and glamours dissipated. By the intelligent presentation of acquired knowledge and facts, the informative mind succeeds in subduing emotion. So often it is found, however, that relatively few people are willing to face true facts unconditionally and without prejudice, because this would mean that cherished misconceptions of the past would have to be recognised and discarded, and to do so would require a degree of mental humility which many do not possess. For mental progress it is therefore essential that the facts of life should be sternly faced and weighed calmly and dispassionately.

The two facets of the mind, that is, the lower concrete mind and the higher spiritual mind, are the two fundamental aspects through which the Soul finds expression in the human kingdom. Through these two channels man is enabled to contact not only the lower kingdoms of nature, but when the consciousness has been sufficiently raised, he is also enabled to bridge the intervening gap and to commune with the higher spiritual realms. The abstract mind contains the attribute of self-awareness, and when this principle is blended with the lower mind, it is responsible for the awakening of self-consciousness in man. It is this consciousness of the Self (the Soul), of which the undeveloped personality still remains largely unaware. It embodies that magnetic principle which over the centuries and through the course of many lives, will consistently exert its attractive influence and will slowly but surely draw the integrated personality back to its Source, back to the realms of spirit.

In the New Age which man is at present entering with hesitant steps, he will be furnished with ever increasing Light. This will radically affect his conditions of living and alter his attitude towards both his fellow men and world affairs in general, resulting in a vast improvement in human relationships.

As man progresses along his Path, the mind becomes ever more perceptive, and in a way is employed as an organ of sense for the unfolding consciousness. The mind therefore is not only a useful instrument for protecting man's personal concerns, but also serves to maintain his identity and to guide his efforts in the required direction. In due course his powers of discrimination will improve, a higher sense of values will be developed, leading to a clearer discerning of the ideal and the spiritual, instead of remaining focused on material values as in the past. This indicates that improved mind control is being achieved, engendering reciprocal activity between the higher and the lower mind, eventually enabling the worker to function at will in either the higher or lower aspects of his being.

6

DISEASE

As man progresses along his Path, it becomes of ever increasing importance that he should occupy a suitable vehicle, properly furnished with the necessary equipment to ensure that the life purpose, as determined by the Soul, can be appropriately fulfilled. When this instrument proves inadequate, whether through disease, deformity or any other insufficiency, thereby failing to perform the required demands and thus to achieve its intended purpose and destiny, then the surrendering of such a defective form to death should certainly not be considered a disaster. As a rule such a withdrawal of life take place at the demand of the Soul, because the need is felt for a more effective vehicle of expression for realising its objectives.

Undesirable subjective conditions are sometimes brought to outer expression as some form of disease. By bringing such defective inner plights to the surface this may lead to a recognition of the hidden emotional and mental deficiencies, thus facilitating the necessary measures for their elimination.

On the other hand, the incidence of disease may also prove to be the first indication that the Soul is preparing its temporary abode with regard to its intended evacuation, which means for the death of the form. This process of withdrawal, characterised by disease, may be stretched out over a long period, with the body gradually deteriorating and dying, or it may develop rapidly and even suddenly, with the Soul freeing itself with a minimum of decay.

It should therefore be clearly realised that disease is not always the evil enemy it is so often made out to be. It may even be regarded as a friend helping to release the Soul from its restrictions. There are therefore instances where disease should be allowed to take its course, thereby opening the portals for the Soul's liberation. In this respect it should always be remembered that as far as the human being is concerned, death is as a rule the result of the planned withdrawal of the Inner Life.

That man is inclined to over-emphasise his disease conditions is only natural, because the interests of the majority of men are still focused on their physical and emotional well-being, with no or only slight awareness of their inner needs – the requirements of the Soul. So often the vicissitudes of the form may provide a considerable contribution towards enriching Soul experience. As the Tibetan points out so succinctly, disease may be regarded as merely a form of transient imperfection, with death as the process of release for refocusing the energy concerned, in preparation for some more advanced activity and the next point of attainment along the steadily unfolding path towards the ultimate objective.

7

THE LIFE PRINCIPLE

Man's vitality is dependent on what is generally known as "the breath of life". When for some reason or other this "breath" is withdrawn, consciousness also departs and death sets in. This spirit of life represents the cohesive force which is responsible for holding together and co-ordinating the various elements of the material body. With its forfeiture the form immediately begins to disintegrate.

The limited comprehension of man can never truly fathom the nature of the life principle, and this concept therefore just has to be accepted as a divine energy with which the form is synthesized, vitalised and animated, finally impelling it to its many forms of activity. Broadly speaking it can, however, be said that the life principle is manifested as Spirit, Soul and matter:

Spirit: The life force is the vital energy providing man with his directing will, his purpose and fundamental incentive, thus giving meaning to his daily existence. It provides man with his vivacity, his will to live, to love, to act, to persist and to evolve. These attributes in man find expression through the mind, which for its lower or physical manifestation functions through the brain.

The *Soul* is the underlying coherent force which determines the quality of life, providing those characteristics which distinguish one individual from the next, and is displayed as man's humours, desires, peculiarities, inclinations and general nature. These distinctive traits are actually the result of the interplay between the innate spirit and the material aspects of the body, equipping man with his subjective nature and his personal attributes.

Matter in the present context refers to those aggregates of atoms or cells composing the members or organs of the physical body. Each atom may be regarded as a separate little life, with its own merits, consciousness and identity, but which are collectively co-ordinated and find expression through the etheric body, which integrates each particular sum-total of atoms into an individualised unit, recognisable by its own specific characteristics.

The life principle will therefore reflect itself throughout the form concerned, but will nevertheless be characterised by some focal point of life expression such as the solar plexus, the heart or the head, which will be determined by the stage of development achieved.

Death marks that point of time when the life force is withdrawn from the physical sheath at behest of the Soul. The region of withdrawal will again depend on the evolutionary stage attained. The two principal exists are firstly the *solar plexus* for those who are still mainly materially biased and astrally orientated, and this will therefore include the greater majority of mankind. The second point of exit is the *head centre*, in the case of those who are more mentally and spiritually attuned. For the average, kindly, well-meaning person, whose life has generally been characterised by goodwill to his fellow men, a third point of withdrawal is also provided, namely from the *heart*. The kind of life that has been led, the point of orientation of the life energies, will therefore exert a considerable influence upon the nature and course of the death process.

THE PROCESS OF DYING

Our entire planetary existence is characterised by rhythmic movement, by coming and going, in-breathing and out-breathing, by periodic creative manifestation in form and a subsequent breaking down of the crystallised energies, restoring the released energies to their vast and ever changing reservoir. These are the universal processes which in the more circumscribed conditions of human existence, are displayed as life and death. It is the interplay of these two elements of being which give rise to the fundamental activity of creation, under the impulsive and guiding force of that Great Being which man knows as God, the Ruler or Logos of our planet.

The human Soul, a fractional component or spark of the One Soul, finds expression through the human kingdom of nature in order to gain physical experience, which eventually will enable him to achieve complete control over the rest of the world of matter. His fear of death arises from the fact that he is temporarily so predisposed towards the material aspects, that he is losing sight of, or even remains totally unaware of his spiritual extraction and that the return to these subjective realms forms his final destiny. This fear will therefore only be dispelled when he becomes better acquainted with what is in store for him after passing beyond the veil and fulfilling the great act of restitution which is commonly known as death. The time is coming when man will clearly recognise the stage when the purpose of the Soul has been fulfilled as far as its present physical incarnation is concerned, and when the Soul's attractive force becomes so potent that the physical instrument will be willingly relinquished for return to its spiritual abode.

Man's existence on the physical plane may be terminated by various causes. There are external circumstances, forming part of the comprehensive Divine Plan, wherein the role played by the puny human being disappears into insignificance, and where the individual free will has to submit its trivial interests to broader and more inclusive schemes, affecting the fortunes of humanity as a whole. Life may for instance be cut short by some sudden catastrophe, originating from a quite unexpected source, thus forcing the Soul to take an abrupt departure without notice or opportunity for preparation.

Normally, however, if such a term may be used in this unpredictable world of ours, the "will to live", or the decision as to when the Thinker intends to withdraw its consciousness from the vehicle it has temporarily occupied in the world of matter, lies with the Soul.

This abstraction of life is effected by the withdrawal of the etheric body, either from the top of the head, from the heart, or from the solar plexus, leaving the dense physical framework without its cohesive principle, and thus allowing it to disintegrate and the component atoms duly to be absorbed into the surrounding physical environment.

While fulfilling its function in the physical body, the etheric body remains linked to it by means of the "Silver Cord", a link of etheric matter with exceptional elastic qualities. This connection has the fantastic property of allowing it to stretch practically beyond all known limits. This attribute is brought into place when the etheric body is temporarily withdrawn, for instance when the Soul uses the etheric body as vehicle during sleep. At such a time the Soul may decide to go on some astral journey which might take the wandering spirit right to the other side of the earth. During such an escapade a remnant of the etheric body is however retained in the physical sheath to ensure that the life processes are not extinguished, and the roving etheric body remains attached to its source by means of the silver cord. This attenuated but nevertheless quite safe connection enables the Soul with its etheric complement to return to its physical abode at a moment's notice. It is only when this cord is somehow severed, that the intimate association between the vital body and its physical counterpart will be disrupted, leaving the lifeless physical instrument to decompose.

All of creation in its innumerable patterns of manifestation, remains subject to a perpetual state of evolution characterised by alternate phases of objective expression and subjective obscuring, again followed by a period when the accent is mainly focused on the subjective life. This can be compared with a process of periodic out-breathing of the Creative Entity, followed by the inevitable sequel of in-breathing. This rhythmic tendency displayed by every form of life, is also evidenced in man by the periodic incarnation of the Soul, submitting itself voluntarily for the sake of experience to the restrictions of a physical vehicle. This temporary instrument will die again after a shorter or longer life, thereby releasing the bonds which temporarily impeded the Soul, allowing it to enjoy a further period of unencumbered sojourn in the subjective realms.

The process of dying can be briefly summarised into four stages:

Firstly, the life force contained in the etheric body is completely withdrawn from the physical form by severing the "silver cord", and allowing the objective body to disintegrate.

Secondly, the life force is next relinquished by the etheric body, which is thereby devitalised and consequently fades out.

Then comes the *third* stage which, depending on the phase of development, is also the last stage in the case of many lives. The vital force released by the etheric body becomes established in the astral vehicle, where it may remain until the Soul is again reincarnated in a physical body. In more advanced instances, the sojourn in the emotional sphere will only be of a temporary nature until the life force is again withdrawn to enter the *Fourth* stage, when the vital force becomes centred in the mental body. With further progress the life force is withdrawn entirely from the various spheres of influence associated with the material existence, and now becomes entirely focused at Soul levels and in the spiritual realms.

9

THE NATURE OF DEATH

One of the main problems of the vast majority of men is the negative attitude they still entertain towards death, inevitably leading to an ever present though perhaps largely unconscious fear of death. The average man still regards the disappearance of life from visual observation in the form, and the subsequent corruption and disintegration of this material body, as an absolute disaster. The reason for this fear is quite understandable, because there is as yet no clear conception of the true nature of death. In the back of the mind there remains that gnawing dread of the biblical picture, imprinted on the mind since early childhood, of burning perpetually in Hell for the major or lesser "sins" committed by each and every normal person during the course of his life.

But those who believe in either purgatory or heaven, already consciously or subconsciously do acknowledge the existence of some form of after-life. Most people have, however, been intimidated to such an extent by the possible consequences of their "sinful" life, and these offences weigh so heavily on their conscience, that few entertain any confidence of going to heaven. To these poor people there only seems to exist the two extremes, of either having to descend to the nethermost regions of hell, with its perpetual fires, or its opposite, a Heaven with golden streets, where the harp-playing angels live on milk and honey. So to most of them death remains a frightful prospect, and the possibility of its closer approach is anticipated with horror and consternation.

Closer acquaintance with the true facts fortunately reveals a totally different picture.

To the average man death remains a catastrophe and a calamity.

It is the abrupt termination of all with which he was familiar, of that which he loved and of his desires, suddenly concluding all his worldly schemes and projects. No matter what his beliefs, there nevertheless remains that gnawing uncertainty about the continuity of life and of that which is awaiting him on the other side. Only rarely will the individual be encountered who no longer just believes in his survival, but who is absolutely convinced and knows that he will pass over with complete retention of consciousness, and that in the subjective worlds he will be able to serve even more effectively than he is able to do at present while still encumbered with physical restrictions. These individuals are in the fortunate position that they can actually look forward with joy in their hearts to that happy moment when the physical vehicle can be finally vacated as the result of the conscious will of the Soul. This time will however only arrive after the task set for the present life has been successfully completed.

Relatively few people are as yet Soul conscious, and consequently the majority do not yet react consciously to the commands of their inner being. It is because the objectives and will of the Soul remain unknown that death at times may appear so absolutely senseless.

Death should actually be regarded as the great Liberator, releasing the spirit aspect either temporarily or permanently from the imprisoning form, depending on the stage of development attained.

Love of life is an entirely natural human instinct, fulfilling a useful function by providing the necessary incentive for preserving and protecting the life concerned. It is this devotion and attachment to life and all it stands for, that underlies a corresponding fear of death. This gnawing dread of the unknown will only begin to fade when there is an awakening awareness that somehow there is a continuity of existence. As more evidence and deeper knowledge is acquired, this awareness of an after-life will gradually develop into certainty and eventually into absolute conviction about the immortality of the human spirit. With a proper understanding of the nature of both life and death, all these needless fears, based on ignorance, emotional impulses and illusion, will be dispelled, and the time may even arrive when there will be a growing feeling of anticipation for the day when the Soul will be allowed to discard these limiting shackles of the material life moving on to the freer subject-ive existence of the hereafter.

Death should be considered as merely incidental, a temporary phase, and as a point of transition in an endless sequence of trans-formations as man moves from stage to stage along his ceaseless path of development. Once the individual becomes profoundly aware of this fact, his whole attitude will become changed, not only with regard to life but also to death. Actually all fear of death will fade away as soon as there is a clear and intelligent understanding of the conditions prevailing beyond "the veil". Man's approach to death should therefore become that of a happy looking forward to that inevitable occasion, with the firm knowledge that a better phase of living may be expected.

In one's association with fellow men there is usually the inclina-tion to avoid the theme of death in conversation. This is a wrong attitude, because it is important that a better understanding of the nature of death should be developed, and this can only be achieved by a sober and intelligent approach and discussion of this matter which so intimately concerns each and everyone. The morbid atti-tude towards the subject of death should be avoided, as it is merely indicative of ignorance about the true state of affairs.

10

LIFE AFTER DEATH

What the average well-meaning person knows as death, is actually nothing but entrance into a fuller and more adequate life, liberated from the many fetters and limitations of the fleshly vehicle, and where life interests will be carried forward with retention of full consciousness. But of course, the nature of death and the conditions to be encountered in the after-life, will vary considerably in accordance with the stage of development attained by the individual.

For the totally unevolved person who has not yet developed an adequate mental body for the storage of memories, and who only lives from day to day trying to satisfy his physical needs, death will be similar to falling into a dreamless sleep, with no recollections to which to react.

A different situation however lies in store for the depraved, the immoral and evil one, for those villains whose sole purpose in life is the satisfying of their selfish and vicious desires. These unfortunates land themselves in a condition which is generally known as "earth-bound". During their earth life their activities were so intensely focused on the material and sensual aspects, that no room was left for developing any spiritual interests, with the consequence that they remained totally unaware of the existence of the subjective worlds. This unilateral and biased state of consciousness will continue after death and with their attention still entirely centred on their material desires and the activities on which they were engaged during the closing stages of their earth life, they will often find it impossible to realise that they have actually passed on to the other side of the curtain. This lack of awareness of their true state of being may result in a hopeless and sometimes desperate struggle to reassert themselves, and to return to their previous field of material exertions. As may well be imaged this impotence to re-establish contact with former associates in their physical environment, might at times prove extremely frustrating.

A rather similar state of attachment to that which is left behind sometimes occurs even in the case of those already somewhat further advanced. There are for example instances where a person feels unable to release or disassociate himself from the self-assumed responsibility of completing some unfulfilled task on which he had been engaged. Or an individual might even be held back by what he considers as unbreakable bonds of love and responsibility.

For those who have definitely entered the path of return, death will simply mean a continuance of those service activities in which they were engaged while still in the physical body, with this difference that they will have a much wider scope, no longer being impeded by the restrictions of the physical sheath.

Where there is an intelligent understanding of the laws governing the processes of death, the person concerned will be able to retain continuity of consciousness by withdrawing in complete and waking awareness from the physical body, and transferring his consciousness to the astral plane. Although such an individual surrenders the instrument he used for contacting the physical world, he will notwithstanding realise that fundamentally and consciously he remains the same, retaining the same states of feeling and of thought-life which qualified his material existence. Although he can no longer communicate with his associates on the astral plane by word of mouth, he finds that his thoughts are imparted even more effectively by telepathic communication. At first this form of intercourse might seem objectionable because others are enabled to read one's inner deliberations like an open book, and secret thoughts can therefore no longer be entertained. Dwellers in the subjective worlds therefore quickly have to adapt themselves to this open-mind condition by purifying their thought-life, retaining only that which is positive, constructive and of a loving nature.

There is no "heaven" for the little evolved. Man is only entitled to that which he has earned during preceding lives. The unevolved therefore does not yet deserve this exalted state, nor has he developed the mentality to appreciate such a condition, and that is why such individuals as a rule only tarry briefly in the subjective worlds before they reincarnate to start their next physical adventure.

In the case of the more advanced, where the personality has experienced a richer and more complete life, but where there is as yet no conscious co-operation with the Soul, shorter or longer periods of joy and rapture may be undergone, depending on the capacity of the man to meditate upon and profit from experiences. But it is only when the stage is reached where the Soul takes complete charge of the personality life and the man's interest is turned from the material to become focused on the higher levels of existence, that he will spontaneously find his way to the portals of "heaven" when passing over.

Because the majority of men are still mainly inclined to limit their attention, their thoughts and activities to physical levels, their after-life in the astral spheres will be characterised only by semiconsciousness and a consequent distorted awareness of their surroundings, resulting in mental and emotional confusion.

It should always be remembered that man's views about hell or heaven are entirely personal and relative, and for the greater part of his functional existence in a physical body his concept of the hereafter will be that of the astral world and therefore illusionary. Similarly it should also be realised that the vast majority of descriptions provided by mediums and clairvoyants also originate from those still moving in astral spheres, although at different levels, and all that they see, experience and record, must therefore be judged accordingly. This means that the views and sentiments expressed must inevitably also be affected by the more or less distorted outlook of the individual concerned. The degree of distortion will depend on the astral level attained, and consequently on the clarity of the Light at his disposal.

D.K.'s teachings are primarily concerned with the ways and means of promoting spiritual development, paying relatively less detailed attention to the intermediate rewards in the after-life which may be earned by such progress. Thee is no doubt, however, that for any achieved improvement there will be a corresponding compensation, even for those still struggling through the murky conditions of the emotional spheres. The main objective is, however, to gain release from this obscure and retarding atmosphere, and to become aware of the brighter light of the spiritual worlds.

The concepts regarding the nature of heaven will therefore vary within wide limits from person to person because the ideas entertained during the early stages will, to a large extent, be figments of the imagination originating from the astral spheres. Only when the worker succeeds in liberating himself from these astral illusions by hesitantly gaining admittance to the unobscured spiritual realms, will a clearer understanding of the true nature of heaven be provided. Actually even before reaching this phase in his development, that is by the time when he arrives at the higher levels of the astral and mental planes, he will already gradually come to the realisation that the true joy to be encountered in the higher worlds, will not consist of walking in celestial cities with golden streets or listening to beautiful angels playing their harps. No, real happiness will only be engendered by the constant rendering of unstinting and loving service to the needful, to those who for one reason or another are still lagging somewhat behind.

No greater joy can be experienced than by unremittingly providing such service day after day, without sleep or rest, no longer being encumbered by any physical restrictions. For man still in the flesh these conditions are difficult to understand, and also that the element of time is really only a product of the physical brain which is registering a state of consciousness determined by the sequence of events on the physical plane. As soon as the individual has rid himself of the material and etheric vehicles, he becomes not only aware of the past and present, but also of the future, and these concepts become timeless to him, all merging into one. Yes, these are thoughts which the normal consciousness cannot yet properly conceive. It is this lack of comprehension, not only of the time factor, but also of other higher dimensions, which makes it so difficult or really impossible for the ordinary earth-bound man to form an adequate picture of that which lies in store for him after passing on.

In considering the question of life after death it should always be clearly realised that whatever the point of reference, this will only be of a transient nature, because man is in a perpetual state of evolution, rhythmically progressing through phases of ebb and flow in accordance with the life beats steadily pulsating through all of creation. And because for each individual the unfolding picture will assume its own dimensions consistent with the specific rays of influence and the varying circumstances to which the entity is subjected, there is not much purpose in trying to describe in detail any particular state of future existence, which will in any case only prove to be a temporary phase or a momentary experience in the constantly changing pattern of the kaleidoscope of life. The afterlife, or existence in the subjective worlds, is just as real and must be regarded as merely a further episode in the ever-evolving life experience of the individual.

The person interested in the thoughts so far expressed with regard to the nature of the hereafter, may rest assured that whether he is aware of the fact or not, he has actually entered the path of return which eventually will lead him back to the "Father's House" – no matter what precise interpretation he may at this stage attach to these stereotyped words. After each reincarnation of the Soul, after each longer or shorter term of experience in a material body, he will return to the subjective worlds as a somewhat wiser man as the result of the additional knowledge acquired through the trials and encounters while temporarily occupying a physical vehicle. During this subsequent residence in the subjective worlds, the newly acquired experiences will be transmuted into innate wisdom, the essence of which will be assimilated in the Soul's ever expanding consciousness. In due course, the need will be felt for supplementary physical adventures and an urge for reincarnation.

And thus the process will be continued steadily, life after life, with the Soul's consciousness step by step gaining in stature, until the time arrives when all possible lessons to be acquired from worldly experience have been learnt, absorbed and stored in the consciousness, without there being any further justification for returning to the physical plane. This, however, does not mean the end of the evolutionary process. By no means, but henceforth this course will proceed on spiritual levels. To begin with, the purified, evolving entity will be absorbed as a junior in the ranks of the Hierarchy of the Masters of Wisdom, where his training in ever more effectively serving humanity and of contributing his minute share towards realising the Divine Plan for the Universe, will systematically be continued over the aeons!

11

CONCLUSION

The object with this book has certainly not been to produce suitable evidence to convince the dubious minded of the existence of an after-life. Far from it. Today, and as far as that is concerned, for many years already, there is such a mass of irrefutable evidence available to the unprejudiced and open-minded investigator, that for these people no further proof is needed. There remains, however, that small minority who will still dispute or simply just deny any form of after-existence. These poor people include the so-called scientists still so hemmed in by their narrow and purblind materialistic criteria that they heedlessly refuse to consider any evidence which cannot be discerned directly by their physical senses or instruments, as well as those perverse minds who "out of principle" refuse even to consider such nonsense as the existence of any subjective realms. What a pity that these unfortunate men are still unaware of what they miss by their short-sighted approach to life, but under the circumstances they will just have to carry on until their eyes will be opened at some later stage – either in the present or some future life. As a rule it may be taken for granted that there is some sound karmic reason for such temporary blindness.

Yes, although the spirit of man is definitely immortal, the question as to the true nature of such after-existence remains a relative enigma. It is in this respect that there still exists a great deal of uncertainty, which is consequently inclined to generate a fear of the unknown and therefore also of death. It is with the hope of throwing a little more light on this subject that some of the basic principles have been discussed and that a few typical descriptions of what may be encountered in the hereafter, have been set out. Actually any number of accounts of what may be seen and experienced on the other side are available from a relatively wide source of literature on the subject. As might be expected each account will, however, differ in detail, but a central corroborative theme nevertheless remains common to practically all of them.

The differences in these descriptions are easily accounted for. In the first instance there are no two individuals who are identically constituted psychically, mentally and spiritually. Each person consequently has his own specific thought life, is influenced by his own particular set of circumstances, and is characterised by the point of development in consciousness attained on his unique evolutionary path. Each one views and classifies that part of the world that is discernable to him by means of his own particular astral and mental complex. The consequence is that any given set of circumstances, observed or experienced by different individuals, will be registered and interpreted in as many distinctive ways, thus giving rise to the widely varying conclusions and reactions, and to constant misunderstandings and friction between man and man.

What further accentuates this disparity in outlook, understanding and performance, is the fact that the vast majority of men are still functioning on emotional or astral levels, thus largely living in a world of illusion, of inadequately controlled emotions engendered by greed, lust, hate and similar expressions of selfishness. It is only when the mental intellect gradually gains precedence over the purely emotional life, that a better and more balanced understanding will be achieved of the prevailing conditions which control the lower worlds of existence.

In the preceding notes the accent has been placed mainly on the nature of the after-life. In this connection it should be clearly kept in mind, however, that these considerations should not be allowed to occupy our minds unduly, and certainly not to the extent of providing us with a perverted perspective of the eventual objectives of each and every life. Viewed from its broader aspects, the nature of our immediate hereafter, no matter from what level this may be recorded, remains but an interlude, a brief and passing phase in the long and extended range of life and death experiences which sequentially constitute the evolutionary history of each individual.

As life follows life, each life period will be succeeded by an after-life, the nature of which will largely be determined by the quality of the preceding existence on earth, and the degree of spiritual progress that has been achieved, finding expression as expansions of consciousness.

No matter at what level of development the aspirant may find himself, such advances in phenomenal living will in each succeeding after-life be characterised by an ever increasing degree of Light by which all that is encountered will be illuminated. Our path thus leads us step by step from material existence to spiritual life, from periodic death to final immortality, from utter darkness to the Supernal Light to be encountered in the House of the Father.

And with the attaining of Light and Wisdom each human being automatically develops his own sphere of influence, and spreads forth his own Light in all directions, thus serving as a connecting link between the Inner Source of Light and the outer regions of darkness where the souls of those still lagging behind are clamouring for illumination. Those who have attained the Light will become centres of vibrant Life, spontaneously radiating their influence to all that surrounds them, vivifying not only fellow human beings to renewed effort, but also furnishing the surrounding animal and vegetable life with fresh energy. May we prove receptive to ever more LIGHT!

THE GREAT INVOCATION

From the point of Light within the Mind of God
Let Light stream forth into the minds of men.
Let Light descend on Earth.

From the point of Love within the Heart of God
Let Love stream forth into the hearts of men.
May Christ return to Earth.

From the centre where the Will of God is known
Let purpose guide the little wills of men –
The purpose which the Masters know and serve.

From the centre which we call the race of men
Let the Plan of Love and Light work out
And may it seal the door where evil dwells.

Let Light and Love and Power restore the Plan on Earth.

"The above Invocation or Prayer does not belong to any person or group but to all Humanity. The beauty and the strength of this Invocation lies in its simplicity, and in its expression of certain central truths which all men, innately and normally, accept – the truth of the existence of a basic Intelligence to Whom we vaguely give the name of God; the truth that behind all outer seeming, the motivating power of the universe is Love; the truth that a great Individuality came to earth, called by Christians the Christ, and embodied that love so that we could understand; the truth that both love and intelligence are effects of what is called the Will of god; and finally the self-evident truth that only through Humanity itself can the Divine Plan work out."

ALICE A. BAILEY

REFERENCE INDEX
BOOKS BY THE TIBETAN
(DJWHAL KHUL)
through ALICE A. BAILEY

Book Ref. No.	Title	First Edition
1.	Initiation, Human and Solar	1922
2.	Letters on Occult Meditation	1922
3.	A Treatise on Cosmic Fire	1925
4.	A Treatise on White Magic	1934
5.	Discipleship in the New Age – Vol. I	1944
6.	Discipleship in the New Age – Vol. II	1955
7.	The Problems of Humanity	1947
8.	The Reappearance of The Christ	1948
9.	The Destiny of Nations	1949
10.	Glamour: A World Problem	1950
11.	Telepathy and the Etheric Vehicle	1950
12.	Education in the New Age	1954
13.	The Externalisation of the Hierarchy	1957

A Treatise on the Seven Rays

14.	Vol. I – Esoteric Psychology I	1936
15.	Vol. II – Esoteric Psychology II	1942
16.	Vol. III – Esoteric Astrology	1951
17.	Vol. IV – Esoteric Healing	1953
18.	Vol. V – The Rays and the Initiations	1960

Published by:
Lucis Trust
Suite 54
3 Whitehall Court
LONDON
U.K., SW1A 2EF

Lucis Trust
113 University Place
11th Floor
NEW YORK
N.Y. 1003
U.S.A.

NOTE

Reference Example: A reference number, such as for instance (12-135/6) at the end of a quotation, would refer to a quotation taken from "Education in the New Age" (12) starting on page 135, and continued on page 136.

Lightning Source UK Ltd.
Milton Keynes UK
UKHW021251090719
345850UK00004B/631/P